THE DREYFUS AFFAIR

А. ДРЕЙФУСЪ   א. דרייפוס   A. DREJFUS

Captain Alfred Dreyfus in 1894 at the age of 35

THE DREYFUS AFFAIR
A TRILOGY

by George R. Whyte

OBERON BOOKS
LONDON

First published in this collection in the United Kingdom in 2010
by Oberon Books Ltd
521 Caledonian Road, London N7 9RH
Tel: 020 7607 3637 / Fax: 020 7607 3629
e-mail: info@oberonbooks.com
www.oberonbooks.com

A catalogue record for this book is available from the British
Library.

ISBN: 978-1-84943-037-1

All images are reproduced by permission of The Dreyfus Society
for Human Rights

Cover photography by Sarah Nathan-Whyte

Cover design by James Illman

Printed in Great Britain by CPI Antony Rowe, Chippenham.

For

Sally

in remembrance

Contents

The Power of Prejudice

'Death to the Jews' drowned the protests of Alfred Dreyfus during his public degradation as he was stripped of his rank, his honour and, ironically, the very ideals which had guided his life – love of the army and devotion to the patrie. His Calvary was to last 12 years and the Dreyfus Affair it precipitated was to become one of the most troubled periods in the history of France, recording for future generations a far-seeing testimony of the social turbulence of the times.

The defeat of France in the Franco-Prussian war dealt a grievous blow to the pride of the nation. The army became the sacred instrument of revenge. It would recapture the lost territories and regain France's honour. It was revered. It was beyond reproach. It was a hallowed institution.

Conversely, the influx of foreigners into France met with increasing antagonism from the population. The country was being invaded by vagabonds, peddlers and upstarts. In an atmosphere of growing xenophobia, the people resented this pollution of their country. The theme of 'Those without a Country' was to be heard again and again counterpointed with 'France for the French'.

Antisemitism, always lurking within a Christian culture, gathered pace when the writer Edouard Drumont, who was to become the 'Pope of Antisemitism', arrived on the scene. The Catholic Church and its organ *La Croix* had long maintained an anti-Jewish stance and the venom of Drumont would take their bigotry to fever pitch. 'To be French was to be Catholic'. Protestants, Freemasons and above all the Jews were suspect.

These three undercurrents, the love of the army, suspicion of the foreigner and mistrust of the Jew, would converge in the Dreyfus Affair and burst the dams of all social restraints creating a torrent of hate on an unprecedented scale.

The conviction of Alfred Dreyfus left many minds unconvinced. The Jewish thinker, Bernard Lazare, was soon to publish his clandestine pamphlet in Belgium. Lucie Dreyfus the loyal wife and Mathieu the 'good' brother began their odyssey for evidence to exonerate Alfred. Theodor Herzl, horrified by the mass hysteria at the degradation, went away to write 'Judenstadt', a manifesto for a Jewish Homeland. Emile Zola, increasingly convinced that there had been a miscarriage of justice, began to voice his doubts and his articles appeared in rapid succession. He deplored that young souls had already been infected by the poison of antisemitism. 'What trepidation for the approaching century.' He implored the youth of France:

> *Oh youth! Youth!*
> *I beg you consider the great task which awaits*
> *you. You are the architects of the future ...*
>
> *Youth! Youth!*
> *Remain always on the side of justice. If the*
> *concept of justice were to fade within your soul,*
> *you will be open to grave dangers.*
>
> *Youth! Youth!*
> *Be humane. Be generous.*

'Where are you heading young people?' he asked, 'towards humanity, truth and justice,' Zola intoned. He was to be ridiculed, mocked and caricatured but became the eloquent spokesman for the cause of justice.

The Jews of France had been stunned into silence, fearing that the shame of one would be visited on them all. In happier times, as Alfred Dreyfus adjusted his uniform every morning, he saw in his mirror the reflection of a proud French Officer. When he arrived at General Staff headquarters he was perceived as a Jewish officer. He did not see or want to see that admission was not acceptance. This was the bitter lesson to be learned from the misfortunes of the assimilationist officer. Jews throughout the world bemoaned the fate of yet one more Jewish martyr while Dreyfus, lingering in his cell on Devil's Island, clutching a small photo of his wife and children, his talisman, ravaged by disease and depression, tortured with a double shackle, tried to hold on to life.

Then came the bombshell, J'Accuse. The sham trial and acquittal of the suspected traitor Esterhazy incensed Zola beyond measure. His 'J'Accuse' roared across the headlines of the newspaper *l'Aurore* on the 13th January 1898 to become the watershed of the Dreyfus Affair. The anti-Dreyfusards closed ranks and the knives were out. Zola would be tried and convicted. He would be abused and vilified. Stripped of his Legion d'Honneur, never to be returned, he was the friend of a traitor (whom he had never met), he was a foreigner in the service of an alleged syndicate, he was in the pay of the Jews. Undaunted, he testified at his trial:

> *Dreyfus is innocent, that I swear. For this I pledge my life for this I pledge my honour.*
>
> *Before France, before the whole world I swear that Dreyfus is innocent, and by my forty years of work, by the authority this labour has given me, I swear that Dreyfus is innocent. And by all that I have gained, by the name which I have made for myself, by my work which has helped to enrich French literature I swear that Dreyfus is innocent. May all this crumble, may all my work perish if Dreyfus is not innocent!*
>
> *He is innocent!*

The Affair had now reached its explosive phase and would engulf the whole country. Its tremors were to be felt throughout the civilised world. Justice was now on trial on the world stage of human rights.

As evidence gathered in favour of Dreyfus, the fight for a re-trial was won and the most intensive period of the Affair was unleashed. At Rennes, the site of the second Court Martial, effigies of Alfred Dreyfus were burnt by uncontrolled mobs. Hatred was mobilised into song with pride of place reserved for the National Hymn converted into 'La Marseillaise Antijuive':

Take up arms Antisemites!	*Aux armes, antijuifs!*
Form your battalions!	*Formez vos battaillons!*
March on!	*Marchons!*
March on!	*Marchons!*
Let their tainted blood	*Qu'un sang impur*
drench our fields!	*abreuve nos sillons.*

Berlin soon responded with 'Dreyfus, Dreyfus über Alles':

Holy Dreyfus, innocent heart	*Heil'iger Dreyfus, Unschuldsseele*
Our pride and joy forever	*Stolz und Stern des ganzen Seins*
Truthful always, never false	*Ohne Falsch und ohne Fehler*
Purity is your endeavour	*Ist Dein Herz, so rein wie kein's!*
Your soul sustains a life so fine	*Nie durchdringt ja Deine Kehle*
No lying and no error	*Dass nichts Unreines sich stehle*
Pig-meat does not pass your lips	*Nu rein bischen Fleisch des Shwein's,*
The thought fills you with terror	*In ein Herz, so rein wie Dein's!*

and endless caricatures, verses and songs were created in an ever more vicious circle of abuse.

The country was in turmoil, society was divided, families were split. Dreyfusards clashed with anti-Dreyfusards. Violence was in the air. Antisemitic riots ravaged the cities of France. Synagogues were ransacked, shops were pillaged, people attacked. Back in Paris Jules Guerin, head of the Antisemitic League was roaming the streets with his People's Army. His headquarters at Fort Chabrol churned out the poisoned pen antisemitic 'L'Antijuive' and became a veritable factory of venom. A whole catechism of calumnies was disgorged by the antisemitic press in an endless series of scurrilous texts as Drumont, at his zenith, prophesised with spine-chilling accuracy:

> *The Jews have to be eternally blind as they have always been not to realise what is awaiting them. They will be taken away as scrap and the people that they oppress so harshly, that they exploit with such ferocity, will dance with joy when they learn that justice has been done.*
>
> *The leader who will suddenly emerge incarnating the idea of an entire nation will do whatever pleases him. He will have the right of life and death. He will be able to employ any means that suit his purpose.*
>
> *The great organiser who will unite the resentments, anger and suffering will achieve a result which will resound throughout the universe. He will return to Europe its prestige for 200 years. Who is to say that he is not already at work?*

With the innocent officer found guilty again at Rennes the anti-Dreyfusards were vindicated but world opinion was outraged. Zola was aghast:

> *I feel terror.*
>
> *The sacred terror of rivers flowing back to their source, of the earth turning without a sun.*

Never has there been a more detestable monument of human infamy or act of wickedness.

It will make future generations shudder.

Dreyfus, convicted a third time by his pardon, continued the fight until his total exoneration and it is to the everlasting credit of France that justice was finally done. Zola died in 'mysterious' circumstances and was both reviled and honoured in his obituaries. His ashes were eventually transferred to the Pantheon where an attempt was made on the life of Alfred Dreyfus. The culprit was acquitted.

Rumblings of the Affair continued and do to this day. The first war passed, with its horrors, to be surpassed by the second with its atrocities. Members of the Dreyfus family fought valiantly, served in the Resistance, died. Nor were the transports from Drancy to Auschwitz to be without a member of the Dreyfus family. The songwriters' predictions were fulfilled. 'Take up arms Antisemites' became a reality as did 'Death to the Jews'.

George R. Whyte

Chronology of the Dreyfus Affair

1859 Alfred Dreyfus born in Mulhouse to an Alsatian Jewish family.

1870 The young boy Dreyfus vows to become a soldier as he watches the German Army march into Mulhouse during the Franco-Prussian war.

1871 Alsace-Lorraine is annexed by Germany.

1872 The Dreyfus family opts for French nationality and after a brief stay in Basel transfers to Paris.

1880 Lieutenant Dreyfus graduates from the Ecole Polytechnique.

1886 The antisemite Edouard Drumont publishes *La France Juive.*

1890 Captain Dreyfus marries Lucie Hadamard.

1891 Colonel Schwarzkoppen appointed Military Attaché at the German Embassy in Paris.

1892 Dreyfus completes 2-year course at the Ecole Superieure de Guerre. Drumont launches the catholic newspaper *La Libre Parole* and denounces Jews in the army.

1893 Dreyfus becomes probationer on the General Staff and the only Jewish officer there.

1894 Dreyfus transferred to Army Intelligence. General Mercier appointed Minister of War.

THE CONDEMNATION

1894 July. Major Esterhazy pays first visit to Schwarzkoppen at the German Embassy and offers his services.

September 1. Bordereau arrives at German Embassy detailing French Military secrets.

End September. Bordereau via Bastian arrives at Army Counter-Intelligence. Dreyfus designated as the traitor, without evidence.

October 14. General Mercier orders handwriting test of Dreyfus but signs warrant for his arrest before the result is known.

October 15. Dreyfus is arrested and incarcerated in the Cherche Midi Military Prison.

December 19/21. Court Martial of Dreyfus conducted in Camera. Henry denounces Dreyfus. Secret dossier containing forged evidence passed by Military to the Judges without the knowledge of the Defence.

December 22. Dreyfus found guilty and condemned to public degradation, exile and imprisonment for life.

1895 January 5. Dreyfus publicly degraded in the courtyard of the Ecole Militaire in front of his fellow officers and an hysterical mob. First public signs of violent antisemitism. Theodor Herzl reporting for the *Neue Freie Presse* in Vienna is alarmed.

13 April. Dreyfus arrives on Devil's Island.

THE YEARS OF EXILE

1895 July 1. Picquart appointed head of Army Counter-Intelligence.

1896 February 14. Theodor Herzl publishes in Vienna *Judenstadt*, an attempt at a modern solution of the Jewish problem.

August. Picquart identifies Esterhazy as author of 'Bordereau'.

September 1. Picquart advises Boisdeffre of Esterhazy's guilt. He is rejected.

September 3. Dreyfus on Devil's Island placed in double boucle (double shackles).

September 15. Picquart meets Gonse and recommends arrest of Esterhazy. He is rejected.

November 10. *Le Matin* publishes facsimile of 'Bordereau'.

November 16. Picquart ordered away from Paris.

1897   February. Supported by the Duc d'Orleans, Jules Guerin organises the League Antisemitique Francais.

November 15. Mathieu advertises Bordereau publicly.

November 25. Zola publishes his first article in support of Dreyfus.

December 13. Zola publishes 'Letter to Youth' calling on young intellectuals to support Dreyfus.

December 15. Mathieu Dreyfus denounces Esterhazy as the author of the Bordereau in an open letter to the Ministry of War.

1898   January 7. Zola publishes 'Letter to France'.

January 10/11. Esterhazy given a sham trial before a Court Martial and acquitted.

January 13. Emile Zola publishes 'J'Accuse' in *l'Aurore*.

January 17. Antisemitic riots throughout France. Jules Guerin's People's Army active. Jewish homes and synagogues besieged, shops broken into. Incidents in Nantes, Bordeaux, Montpelier, Tours, Toulouse. Dreyfus effigies burnt. Demonstrations in Marseille, Nancy and all of Lorraine. Religious services held to continue the 'sacred battle' against the Jews. In Algeria synagogues ransacked. Jews stoned.

January 24. von Bulow declares in Reichstag that Germany never had contact with Dreyfus.

February 7/23. Zola tried for Libel and declared guilty. Fined and sentenced to one year in prison. Later flees to England.

February 26. Picquart dismissed from the Army.

February 28. Lucie Dreyfus requests permission to go to Devil's Island but is refused.

March 4. Picquart, Henry duel. Henry slightly wounded.

July 7. Minister of War Cavaignac unknowingly reads to the Chamber of Deputies, as a proof of Dreyfus's guilt, one of Henry's forgeries.

July 13. Picquart arrested.

August 30. Henry confesses to forging documents and is imprisoned.

August 31. Henry found dead in his prison cell.

September 1. Esterhazy flees to England.

September 3. Cavaignac resigns. Lucie Dreyfus petitions for a re-trial.

THE RETRIAL

1899   June 3. United Court of Appeal revokes 1894 verdict and orders Dreyfus to be re-tried by Court Martial in Rennes.

June 5. Zola returns to France.

June 9. Dreyfus sets sail for France.

June 9. Picquart is freed.

August 7 to September 9. Rennes Trial. Dreyfus declared guilty and condemned to Public Degradation and 10 years of prison.

September 19. At the instigation of his family who fear for his survival, Dreyfus accepts pardon to enable him to prove his innocence.

1900 April 14. Exposition Universelle opens in Paris.

1902 September 2. Zola dies 'mysteriously' at home from asphyxiation. Later evidence indicates foul play.

THE REHABILITATION

1903 April 4. Jean Juares demands in the Chamber of Deputies revision of Rennes verdict.

1906 July 12. The Supreme Court of Appeal in Paris annuls the Rennes verdict and declares Dreyfus innocent of all the charges against him.

July 13. Parliament votes to reinstate Dreyfus and Picquart into the Army.

July 21. Dreyfus is awarded the Legion of Honour at a public ceremony.

October 15. Dreyfus resumes military duties.

October 25. Clemenceau becomes Prime Minister. Picquart is appointed Minister of War.

1908 June 4. Zola's ashes are transferred to the Pantheon. Attempt on the life of Dreyfus during the ceremony. Culprit is acquitted.

1914 January 19. Picquart dies in riding accident.

July 31. Jean Jaures, socialist Dreyfusard statesman, assassinated.

August 2. Dreyfus returns to active duty, promoted Lieutenant Colonel and serves in first world war.

1931 February. The Paris Theatre Nouvel-Ambigu presents *L'Affaire Dreyfus* by the German writers Reifish and Herzog in a French version – attacked by the right wing *l'Action Francaise.* Violent demonstrations, arrests and wounded.

1935 July 12. Death of Alfred Dreyfus, buried in the Cemetery of Montparnasse in Paris.

1945 December 14. Death of Lucie Dreyfus.

1988 June. Erection of statue to Dreyfus in the Jardin de Tuileries after its refusal at the Ecole Militaire. June. Desecration of the grave of Dreyfus in the Cemetery of Montparnasse.

1994 Commemorations of the Dreyfus Centenary.

Principal Characters

BASTIAN, MARIE-CAUDRON

Becomes cleaner at the German Embassy in Paris in 1889 and eventually the concierge; works as agent for French Army Intelligence in particular passing fragments of documents and papers found in wastepaper baskets at the embassy for 200 francs per month; in contact with Henry to whom she passes the 'bordereau'.

BOISDEFFRE, GENERAL RAOUL FRANÇOIS LE MOUTON, CHARLES DE

Born 1839; Army Chief of Staff from 1893 to 1898; fervent Catholic; ignores Picquart's protestations; resigns after Henry's confession of forgeries; dies 1919.

DREYFUS, CAPTAIN ALFRED

Born in Mulhouse on 9 October 1859 to Jeannette and Raphael Dreyfus, industrialist, the seventh and youngest child; the Alsatian Jewish family embarks on a course of assimilation, loosening its ties to Judaism in order to strengthen its ties with France; enters Ecole Polytechnique in 1878; Lieutenant 1882; Captain 1889; at Ecole de Guerre 1890-92; leaves 1892; ninth in his class with a mention of très bien; joins general staff of Ministry of War in 1893 where he is the only Jewish officer; marries Lucie Hadamard in 1890; his son Pierre is born in 1891 and his daughter Jeanne in 1893.

DREYFUS, LUCIE

Wife of Alfred; born Lucie Hadamard in 1871 and of a more traditional Jewish background than her husband; observes Jewish Holy Days and is dedicated to biblical study; accomplished pianist; exhibits unshakeable loyalty to her husband throughout the Affair; in later life devotes much of her time to Jewish causes.

DREYFUS, MATHIEU

Brother of Alfred Dreyfus; born 1857; industrialist; elegant and of distinguished bearing; from 1894 devotes his life to the rehabilitation of his brother Alfred; advertises handwriting of 'bordereau' and is contacted by the banker Castro who identifies it as that of his client Esterhazy; he denounces Esterhazy as the author of the 'bordereau'.

DRUMONT, EDOUARD

Born in 1844; antisemitic leader and writer; writes *La France Juive* in 1886, a tirade against Jews that sells 200000 copies; forms National Antisemitic League in 1899; launches the Catholic *La Libre Parole* in 1892 with a violent campaign against Jews and their admission into the army; becomes the leading organ of antisemitism and anti-Dreyfusard propaganda during the Affair; labelled the 'Pope of Antisemitism'; dies in 1917.

ESTERHAZY, MARIE-CHARLES-FERDINAND

Born in Paris in 1847; illegitimate descendant bearing the name of the Esterhazy family; becomes Papal Guard and then joins the Foreign Legion; marries in 1887 the daughter of the Marquis de Nettancourt; always in financial difficulties; takes Marie Pays a young prostitute as his mistress; calls on Schwartzkoppen in 1894 to offer his services; is relieved of duty after Henry's confession of forgeries on 30 August 1898; escapes to England and admits writing the 'bordereau'; he lives in England under the name of Count Jean de Voilement and dies in Harpenden, Hertfordshire in 1923; receives regular sums at the local post office, from an unknown source.

GONSE, GENERAL CHARLES ARTHUR

Born in 1838; Deputy Chief of Staff; strong anti-Dreyfusard; friend of Boisdeffre; refuses to listen to Picquart's evidence against Esterhazy; replaced after Henry's confession; dies 1917.

GUERIN, JULES

Active antisemite; supported by the Duc d'Orléans; founds the Ligue Antisémitique in 1897; publishes *L'Antijuif*; masterminds street violence with his People's Army; establishes his headquarters at Ford Chabrol in Paris and is eventually disgraced.

HENRY, MAJOR HUBERT JOSEPH

Born in 1846; volunteers for the army in 1865; becomes Second Lieutenant in 1870 and Captain in 1879; wounded in the Franco-Prussian War; Legion d'Honneur 1895; Lieutenant-Colonel 1897; gives false testimony at first Dreyfus trial and creates forgeries to strengthen the army's case against Dreyfus; confesses to the forgeries during intensive interrogation by Minister of War Cavaignac on 30 August 1898; found dead in his prison cell the following day.

MERCIER, GENERAL AUGUSTE

Born in 1833; participates in the campaigns of Mexico and Metz; Colonel in 1883; General de Brigade in 1885; becomes Minister of War in 1894; masterminds creation of sham secret dossier handed furtively to the judges at the first Dreyfus court-martial to influence their decision; gives virulent anti-Dreyfus testimony in Rennes; remains implacable foe of Dreyfus until the end of his life; dies in Paris in 1921.

PATY DE CLAM, MARQUIS DU

Born in 1853; General Staff Officer; designated as Officer of Judiciary Police on 14 October 1894; masterminds enquiry against Dreyfus and invents the scenario of his hostile interrogation and handwriting test; Lieutenant-Colonel in 1896; participates in intrigues with Esterhazy on behalf of the Military; theatrical personality; dies in 1916. Son appointed head of Jewish Bureau under Vichy government.

PAYS, MARGUERITE-MARIE

Young and attractive prostitute from the provinces whom Esterhazy reputedly met on a train journey to Paris or at the Moulin Rouge; is already well-known in her profession at the age of 19; intelligent and loyal to Esterhazy; becomes his mistress.

PICQUART, LIEUTENANT-COLONEL MARIE-GEORGES

Born in Strasbourg in 1854; Saint Cyr; Ecole de Guerre; outstanding officer; exhibits antisemitic traits; promoted Head of Counter-Intelligence in 1895; Lieutenant-Colonel in 1896; becomes suspicious of Esterhazy and denounces him; as a result falls into conflict with his senior officers Generals Boisdeffre and Gonse; relieved of his duties in February 1898; arrested in July 1898 and incarcerated at La Santé and then Cherche-Midi Prison until June 1899; re-integrated into the army with the rank of brigadier-general in 1906 following the rehabilitation of Dreyfus; appointed Minister of War in the Clemenceau Government in 1906; multilingual of exceptional intellect; accomplished musician and pianist; forms Mahler Society; dies in 1914 from a riding accident.

SCHWARTZKOPPEN, COLONEL MAXIMILIEN VON

Born in 1850 in Potsdam; enters the Infantry Regiment of Westphalia in 1868; participates in the Franco-Prussian War 1870; Captain in 1882; Commandant in 1888; appointed Military Attaché at German Embassy in Paris 1891; has contact with Esterhazy from 1894; participates in the First World War as Commander of the 20th Infantry Division; dies from wounds in hospital in Berlin 1917, affirming the innocence of Dreyfus whom he had never met.

ZOLA, EMILE

French novelist born in Paris in 1840; family of Italian origin; begins to take interest in the plight of Dreyfus in 1897 and his articles appear in rapid succession with *Lettre à la Jeunesse* in December 1897 and *Lettre à la France* on 6 January 1898; his letter to the President of France, entitled *J'Accuse* appears in *L'Aurore* on 15 January 1898 accusing the General Staff of conspiracy to convict Dreyfus; tried for libel and convicted in February 1898 and sentenced to a fine and one year in prison; he takes refuge in Britain; he dies 'mysteriously' of asphyxiation at his home in 1902; his remains are transferred to the Pantheon in 1908.

Emile Zola

Prologue: My Burning Protest

by George Whyte after Emile Zola

What G-d reigns over us?
What morals guide us?

Never has an assassin
Never has a man insane
been so closely guarded.
The eternal silence
the slow agony
the curse of a whole people.

A hidden poison
has led us to delirium.
Hatred for the Jew
there lies the guilt
the daily ritual
recited year in year out
in the name of morality
in the name of Christ.

This barbaric campaign
a mirror of dark ages
shatters our brotherhood
and horrifies my passion
for tolerance and justice.

What is more simple
what is more natural
then to expose the truth?

But here is the black soul
the abominable figure
the traitor
who sells his brothers
as Judas sold his G-d.

And,
if no reason is found
to explain the crime
is it not enough
that he is a Jew?

Now,
dare you say
he is innocent?

Ah! when I was young
I saw
the passions of youth
its love of freedom
and hatred of force
which crushes the soul.

Now fresh minds
infected by this poison
greet a new century
declaring
they will massacre all the Jews
for they are another race
another faith.
What horror this portends
at the dawn
of the new century.

Oh Youth! Dear Youth!
be human
be generous
strive for the cause of justice
for who will
if not you?

Youth! Dear Youth!
I beg you
think of the great task
which awaits you.
If the glow of justice
fades inside you
you could fall victim
to great danger

Youth! Dear Youth!
and you dear students
where are you heading
roaming through the streets
cleansing our discords
with the passions and hope
of your twenty years?

We are marching towards humanity
*   towards truth*
*   towards justice!*

France!

In these frightful days
of moral strife
when consciences darken
dear France I speak to you
to the Nation
to the Homeland.

I will dare speak all
for my passion
is the truth
and the truth is on the march
nothing will stop it.

France
how have your people
succumbed to such fear
and sunk to such depth
of bigotry.
Beware
you are heading to dictatorship
to the Church of the past
with its prejudice and dogma.

France
you have allowed
the rage of hatred
to lash the face of your people
poisoned and fanatic
they scream in the streets
Down with the Jews!
Death to the Jews!

What anguish
what sadness
in the souls of those
who love you.

Dear France
I beg of you
examine your conscience
return to yourself
to the great power
you are.

France! Awake!
Think of your glory
be fair
be generous
whatever assails your reason now
you are the future
and you will awake
in the glory
of truth and justice.

President of the Republic!

A court has acquitted
one who is guilty
and spat in the face
of all truth and justice.

I will then tell the truth
as I have pledged
if the courts of justice
so empowered
did not.

It is my duty to speak
for I will not conspire
to abet a crime
My night would be haunted
by the spectre
of an innocent
his frightful torture
for a crime
he did not commit.

Monsieur le President
it is to you I proclaim the truth
it is to you I turn
in revolt
and with all the force
of an honest man.

Oh the empty accusation!
To condemn a man thus
is a miracle of iniquity.
What a spectacle
what infamy
a man
weighed down with debts and crime
is proclaimed innocent
while the soul of honour
a man without stain
is dragged in the mire.
A country which has come to this
must collapse and decay.

Honest folk
I challenge you
read it and know it
your hearts will pound
with anger and revolt
when you think
of that fearful suffering
on Devil's Island
for the vanity of honoured men
who grind their boots
into the nation
stabbing its throat
as it cries out for truth
their hideous excuse
for reasons of state!
But, the truth grows
when buried underground
it gathers a force
so violent
that the day it bursts
it carries all with it.

The truth is on the march
and nothing will stop it!

Monsieur le President!

I accuse the Ministers of War, the courts, the
Generals and their staff and all who collaborated
with them

I accuse them
of being the diabolical agents
of a judicial error
and defending their deadly work
with revolting cunning.

I accuse them
of suppressing the proof
of a man's innocence
of inhumanity and injustice
to save their face.

I accuse them
of being scoundrels
holding an inquest
of monstrous partiality.

I accuse them
of lying and of fraud
of leading a vile campaign
to mislead the public
and hide their sins.

I accuse them
of violating all human rights
by condemning a man
on testimony kept from him.

I accuse them
of concealing this illegal act
and acquitting a man
they know is guilty.

I have but one passion
a passion for light
in the name of humanity
that has suffered
and has a right
to happiness.
My burning protest
is the cry of my soul
Let them dare
and take me to the courts
let us all be tried
in the full light of day.

I am waiting.

Dreyfus' prison enclosure on Devil's Island, with fortified watch tower

Daniel Mangisch as Dreyfus
in the Zurich production of *Dreyfus Intime*

Photo: Opernhaus Zurich

DREYFUS INTIME

Dreyfus Intime was first performed at the Opernhaus Zurich on 22nd December 2007 with the following cast:

ALFRED DREYFUS   Daniel Mangisch
LUCIE DREYFUS   Aniko Donath
EMILE ZOLA/NARRATOR   Rolf Sommer

Director, George Whyte
Stage Design, Jörg Zielinski
Make-up, Wolfgang Witt
Music, 19th-century piano compositions relating to the
Dreyfus Affair
Piano, Sarah Tysman
Advisor to production, David Poutney

EPISODE 1

PROLOGUE 1

NARRATOR: *(The narrated texts are read sitting, the Zola texts are declaimed standing by the same actor.)*

Paris, 20 November 1943.

From the Commander in Chief of the Security Police in the district of the Military Commander in France.

From SS Obersturmführer Röthke to SS Obersturmbannführer Eichmann. For urgent attention.

"On 20 November 1943 at 11.50 hours Transport train D 901 departed from Paris-Bobigny station, destination Auschwitz. The cargo comprised:

7800 kg	potatoes
300 kg	margarine
420 kg	salt
330 kg	cereals, farinaceous food
600 kg	tins of vegetables
1200	Jews"
	amongst them was Madeleine the grandchild of Alfred and Lucie Dreyfus.

The signpost to this tragedy was engraved throughout the centuries and unveiled at the time of the Dreyfus Affair.

PROLOGUE 2

NARRATOR: Dreyfus was a young French Officer – a Jew – convicted on false evidence in 1894 for a crime of treason of which he was innocent. He was stripped of his rank, publicly degraded and banished to Devil's Island where he was imprisoned under inhumane conditions. Emile Zola took up his cause and his letter to the President of France 'J'ACCUSE' has become history's most famous plea for human rights.

The fight for Dreyfus' innocence lasted 12 years. The Affair rocked France, split the country and unleashed racial hatred. Its repercussions were felt world-wide for decades to come and continue to this day.

MUSIC 1

Captain Alfred Dreyfus was arrested on the 15th of October 1894. He writes to his wife Lucie from his cell in the prison of Chèrche-Midi in Paris.

EPISODE 2

DREYFUS: My dear Lucie,

At last I am able to write you a word. I have just been informed that my trial takes place on the 19th of this month. I am not allowed to see you.

I will not describe to you all that I have suffered; there are no terms in the world strong enough in which to do so.

Do you remember when I used to say to you how happy we were? All of life smiled upon us. Then suddenly came a terrible thunderclap, from which my brain is still reeling. I, accused of the most monstrous crime that a soldier could commit! Even now I think I am the victim of a terrible nightmare.

The truth will come to light at last. My conscience is calm and tranquil, it reproaches me with nothing. I have always done my duty; I have never wavered. I have been overwhelmed, prostrated in my dark prison, alone with my thoughts. I have had moments of wild madness, I have been light-headed even, but my conscience kept watch. It said to me: 'Lift up your head and look the world in the face. Supported by your conscience, walk straight on and right yourself. This is a terrible experience, but you must submit to it.'

I will not write at greater length, for I want this letter to leave this evening.

I embrace you a thousand times, for I love you, I adore you.

A thousand kisses to the children. I dare not speak more to you of them; tears come to my eyes when I think of them.

NARRATOR: The Prison of Chèrche-Midi, two weeks later.

DREYFUS: My darling,

At last I am reaching the end of my sufferings, the end of my martyrdom. Tomorrow I shall appear before my judges, my head held high, my soul at rest.

The experience I have just gone through, a terrible experience though it was, has purified my soul. I shall return to you better than I used to be. I want to consecrate all that remains to me of life to you, to my children, to our dear relatives.

I am ready to appear before soldiers as a soldier who has nothing to reproach himself with. They will see my face, they will read my soul, they will gain the conviction of my innocence, like all those who know me.

Devoted to my country, to which I have consecrated all my strength, all my intelligence, I have nothing to fear. Sleep peacefully, then, my darling, and have no care. Think only of the joy which will be ours when we find ourselves shortly in each other's arms, quickly forgetting these sad and sombre days ...

MUSIC 2 starts.

Awaiting that happy moment, I send you a thousand kisses.

MUSIC 2 ends.

EPISODE 3

NARRATOR: Saturday 22nd of December 1894. Court Martial of the military government of Paris.

Seven judges preside.

In the name of the French people!

Is Captain Dreyfus guilty of having delivered military secrets to a foreign power in order to wage war against France?

Guilty Guilty Guilty Guilty Guilty Guilty Guilty

Yes, by unanimous vote the accused is guilty.

Alfred Dreyfus you are sentenced to deportation, lifelong imprisonment in a fortified enclosure and public degradation.

LUCIE: What a misfortune, what torture, what disgrace! We are all terrified, crushed by it. I know how brave you are, I admire you. You are an unhappy martyr. I entreat you, bear these new tortures bravely still. Our life, the fortune of all of us, shall be devoted to seeking out the guilty. We will find them – we must! You shall be rehabilitated.

DREYFUS: My darling,

I suffer much, but I pity you more than I do myself. I know how you love me; your heart must bleed. On my side, my loved one, my thoughts are always with you, day and night.

To be innocent, to have led a blameless life, and to be convicted of the most monstrous crime that a soldier can commit – what can be more dreadful? It sometime seems to me that I am the plaything of a horrible nightmare.

It is for you alone that I have borne it until now; it is for you alone, my loved one, that I have endured this long martyrdom. Will my strength allow me to continue until the end? I know not. You alone can give me courage; it is from your love that I hope to derive it.

I will try, then, to live for you, but I need your aid.

What is of the first importance is, no matter what becomes of me, to seek out the truth, to move heaven and earth to discover it, to invest all of our means, to rehabilitate my name that has been dragged in the mire. The undeserved stain must be washed out at all costs.

I have not the courage to write to you at greater length. Embrace your dear parents, our children, and everyone for me.

Try to get permission to see me. It seems to me they cannot refuse it to you now.

LUCIE: My dear husband,

You know that I love you, that I adore you, my own dear husband; our intense grief, the horrible infamy of which we are the object, do nothing but tighten the links of my affection.

Wherever you go, wherever they send you, I will follow you;

We shall bear exile more easily together, we will live for each other...; we will educate our children, we will give them a soul well fortified against the vicissitudes of life.

I cannot do without you, you are my consolation; the only gleam of happiness that is left me is to finish my days by your side. You have been a martyr, and you have still to suffer horribly. The punishment which will be inflicted on you is odious. Promise me that you will bear it bravely.

You are strong in your innocence; accept the unmerited punishment; do it for me, for the wife who loves you. Give her this proof of affection, do it for your children; they will be grateful to you one day. The poor children embrace you, and often ask for their papa.

MUSIC 3 starts.

Once more, courage! You must live for our children, for me.

MUSIC 3 ends.

LUCIE: I suffer beyond anything that you can imagine on account of the horrible tortures that you are undergoing; my thoughts do not leave you for a moment. I see you alone in your sad prison, a prey to the most gloomy reflections; I compare our years of happiness, the sweet days we spent together, with the present time. How happy we were, how good and devoted you were to me! With what perfect devotion you cared for me when I was ill, what a father you have been to our poor darlings! All this passes and repasses in my mind; I am unhappy at not having you with me, at being alone. My dear loved one, we must, we absolutely must, be together again; we must live for each other, for we cannot exist without each other.

I weep and weep, and then weep again. Your letters alone bring me consolation in my great grief; they alone sustain me and comfort me. Live for me, I entreat you, my dear friend; gather up your strength, and strive – we will strive together until the guilty man is found.

I am asking an enormous sacrifice of you, that of living for me, for our children, of striving for reinstatement ... I should die of grief if you were no more, I should not have the strength to continue a struggle for which you alone of all the world can strengthen me.

Go through the sad ceremony bravely, raise your head and proclaim your innocence, your martyrdom, in the faces of your executioners.

DREYFUS: I am told that the supreme degradation takes place the day after tomorrow. I was expecting it, I was prepared; nevertheless, the shock was great. I will resist, as I promised you. I will derive the strength that is still necessary for me from your love, from the affection of all of you, from the thought of my darling children, from the supreme hope that the truth will be brought to light. But I must feel that your affection is radiating all around me, I must feel that you are striving with me. So continue your researches without pause or rest.

LUCIE: How I love you, my good darling! Let us hope that all this will come to an end some time. I must husband all my strength.

EPISODE 4

NARRATOR: Saturday 5th of January 1894.

The courtyard of the Ecole Militaire in Paris.

Dreyfus, under guard, is greeted by an hysterical mob:

Death to the traitor! Death to Judas!

(DREYFUS stands to attention.)

Alfred Dreyfus, you have been found guilty of the crime of high treason. You are no longer worthy to bear arms. In the name of the French people we degrade you.

(DREYFUS turns. The back of his uniform is branded with a J.)

DREYFUS: Soldiers, an innocent man is degraded. Soldiers, an innocent man is dishonoured! Vive la France! Vive l'Armée!

NARRATOR: Death to the traitor. Death to the Jews.

DREYFUS: I am innocent! Innocent!

(DREYFUS turns. His tunic is dishevelled.)

LUCIE: My dearest,
What a horrible morning; what atrocious moments! No, I cannot think of it; it causes me too much suffering. I cannot realise that you, my poor friend, a man of honour, you who adore France, you whose soul is so good, whose sentiments are so noble, should suffer the most infamous

41

punishment that can be inflicted on mortal man. It is abominable.

DREYFUS: The first day

My darling,

I have just had a moment of terrible weakness, of tears mingled with sobs, my whole body trembling with fever. It was the reaction after the terrible tortures of the day. It was to be, I felt it; but alas! instead of being allowed to weep in your arms, to lay my head upon your breast, my sobs have echoed only in the emptiness of my prison.

Alas! why cannot the human heart be laid open by a knife so that the truth it contains may be read. Then all the honest, worthy people who have crossed my path would have said to themselves, 'This is a man of honour!' But it is easy to understand their feelings; in their place, I could not have restrained my contempt for an officer who, I was assured, was a traitor. But alas! that is the pity of it; there *is* a traitor, but I am not the man.

LUCIE: My darling husband,

I cannot tell you how grief-stricken I am at the thought of your sufferings. Oh, heaven! what martyrdom.

I think only of you, I will live only for you, and in the hope that we may soon be reunited. Tell me, I entreat you, all you feel, and the state of your health. I have terrible fears that you will break down; oh, if I could only see you, if I could be with you, to try to make you forget a little your misfortune. What would I not give for such a joy!

MUSIC 4 starts.

LUCIE: Here I am again sitting at my desk, lost in my thoughts – in a Reverie.

MUSIC 4 ends.

EPISODE 5

DREYFUS: The 14th day.

My dear Lucie,

On Thursday evening I was roused from my sleep to set out for this place, where I only arrived last evening. I will not tell you about my journey for fear of breaking your heart; suffice it to say that I have heard the justifiable cries of a nation against one whom it thinks a traitor, that is to say, the basest of the base. I no longer know whether I have a heart.

I do not know on whom or what to fix my ideas. When I review the past, anger rushes to my brain; it seems so impossible that I should have been bereft of everything; when I think of my present situation it is so miserable that I look upon death as on the forgetfulness of everything; it is only when I turn towards the future that I have a moment of consolation.

The other day, when I was insulted at La Rochelle, I wanted to escape from my warders, to present my naked breast to those to whom I was a just object of indignation, and say to them: 'Do not insult me; my soul, which you cannot know, is free from all stain; but if you think I am guilty, come take my body, I give it up to you without regret.' Then, perhaps, when under the stinging bite of physical pain, I had cried 'Vive la France!' they might have believed in my innocence!

But what am I asking for night and day? Justice! Justice!

LUCIE: Emile Zola, Letter to France.

ZOLA:
France!
In these frightful days
of moral strife
when consciences darken

dear France I speak to you
to the Nation.
to the Homeland.

I will dare speak all
for my passion
is the truth
and the truth is on the march
nothing will stop it.

France
how have your people
succumbed to such depths
of bigotry?
Beware
you are heading to dictatorship
to the Church of the past
with its prejudice and dogma.

France
you have allowed
the rage of hatred
to lash the face of your people
poisoned and fanatic
they scream in the streets
Down with the Jews!
Death to the Jews!

What anguish
what sadness
in the souls of those
who love you.

Dear France
I beg of you
examine your conscience
return to yourself
to the great power
you are.

France! Awake!
Think of your glory
be fair
be generous
whatever assails your reason now
you are the future
and you will awake
in the glory
of truth and justice.

MUSIC 5.

EPISODE 6

LUCIE: My dear husband,

I cannot tell you the sadness and the grief I feel while
you are going farther and farther away; my days pass in
anxious thoughts, my nights in frightful dreams; only the
children, with their pretty ways and the pure innocence of
their souls, succeed in reminding me of the one compelling
duty I must fulfil, and that I have no right to give way.

I read this morning, the story of your arrival on Devil's
Island according to the newspapers, but although the
news has reached France, I have so far received absolutely
nothing from you. I cannot tell you what my sufferings are,
thus separated completely from the husband whom I so
love, totally deprived of news, and not knowing how you
are bearing up.

Since your departure from France my suffering is doubled;
nothing can equal the fearful anxiety which tortures me.
I should be a thousand times less wretched if I could be
with you. I should at least know how you are, the state of
your health and your energy, and on this score my anxiety
would be at rest.

Provided, Oh God! that the existence awaiting you there
be not too terrible, that you may not be deprived of what is

absolutely necessary, and that you may be able to endure the rigorous treatment inflicted on you.

DREYFUS: Devil's Island, 110th day.

Today I begin the diary of my miserable and terrible existence. Until now I have had faith in reason, I have believed in the logic of things and events, I have trusted in human justice! Nothing strange or unrealistic has found an abiding place in my mind. Oh, what a crumbling away of all my beliefs and all sound reason!

I thought that, once in my exile, I might find, if not rest – at least some tranquillity of mind and body which might permit me to wait for the day of rehabilitation. What a new and bitter disappointment!

When I landed, I was locked in a cell of the prison, with closed shutters, prohibited from speaking to any one, alone with my thoughts, subjected to the regimen of a convict.

Several times I nearly lost my reason; I had congestion of the brain, and my horror of life was such that the thought came to me to refuse medical aid, and thus court the welcome death which would end my martyrdom. This would indeed have been deliverance and the cessation of my long agony, for I should not have broken my promise, and my death would have been only natural.

Oh, how I long to live until the day of rehabilitation, to let the world know my sufferings and give peace to my aching heart. Shall I bear up until that day dawns? I often have doubts, my heart is so broken and my health so shaken.

NARRATOR: October 5, 1895 Dreyfus addresses following letter to the President of the Republic:

"Monsieur le President,

Accused and then found guilty on the sole evidence of handwriting, of the most infamous crime which a soldier can commit, I have declared, and I declare once again, that

I did not write the letter which was imputed to me, and that I have never forfeited my honour.

For a year I have been struggling alone, with a clear conscience, against the most terrible calamity which can befall a man.

I do not speak of physical sufferings; they are nothing; the sorrows of the heart are everything.

To suffer thus is dreadful in itself, but to feel that my dear ones are suffering with me, is horrible. It is the agony of a whole family, expiating an abominable crime which I never committed.

I do not beg for pardon, or favours, or compassion; I only ask, I implore, that full and complete light may be shed upon this machination of which my family and I are the unhappy and miserable victims.

In the name of my honour, torn from me by an appalling error, in the name of my wife, in the name of my children – I ask justice from you; and this justice, which I beg of you with all my soul, with all the strength of my heart, with hands joined in supreme prayer, is to probe the mystery of this tragic history, and thus to put an end to the martyrdom of a soldier and of a family to whom their honour is their all.

MUSIC 6.

EPISODE 7

DREYFUS: It is impossible for me to sleep. This cage, before which the guard walks up and down like a phantom in my dreams, the torment of the vermin which infest me, the smouldering in my heart that I, who have always and everywhere done my duty, should be in this horrible place – all this excites and agitates my nerves, which are already shattered, and drives away sleep. When shall I again pass a calm and tranquil night? Perhaps not until I am in the grave, when I shall sleep the sleep that is ever-lasting. How sweet it will be to think no longer of human vileness and cowardice!

245th day.

The ocean, which I hear moaning beneath my little window, has always for me a strange fascination. It soothes my thoughts as it did before, but now they are very bitter and sombre. It recalls dear memories to mind, the happy days I have passed at the seaside, with my wife and darling children.

I have again the violent sensation which I felt on the ship, of being drawn almost irresistibly towards the sea, whose murmuring waves seem to call to me, like some great comforter. This mysterious influence of the sea over me is powerful; on the voyage from France I had to close my eyes and call up the image of my wife to avoid yielding to it.

Where are the bright dreams of my youth and the ambitions of my manhood? Nothing longer lives within me; my brain wanders under the stress of my thoughts. What is the hidden mystery of this drama? Even now I comprehend nothing of what has passed. To be condemned without palpable proof, on the strength of a forged scrap of handwriting!

Each night I dream of my wife and children. But what fearful awakenings! When I open my eyes and find myself in this wretched cell, I have a moment of such anguish that I could close my eyes forever, never to see or think again.

The air is thick and heavy, the sky black as ink. A genuine day of death and burial.

ZOLA:
What G-d reigns over us?
What morals guide us?

Never has an assassin
Never has a man insane
been so closely guarded.
The eternal silence
the slow agony
the curse of a whole people.

A hidden poison
has led us to delirium.
Hatred for the Jew
there lies the guilt
the daily ritual
recited year in year out
in the name of morality
in the name of Christ.

This barbaric campaign
a mirror of dark ages
shatters our brotherhood
and horrifies my passion
for tolerance and justice.
What is more simple
what is more natural
than to expose the truth?
But here is the black soul
the abominable figure
the traitor
who sells his brothers
as Judas sold his G-d.

And,
if no reason is found
to explain the crime
is it enough
that he is a Jew?

Honest folk
I challenge you
read it and know it
your hearts will pound

with anger and revolt
when you think
of that fearful suffering
on Devil's Island
for the vanity of honoured men
who grind their boots
into the nation
stabbing its throat
as it cries out for truth
their hideous excuse
for reasons of State!
But, the truth grows
when buried underground
it gathers a force
so violent
that the day it bursts
it carries all with it.

DREYFUS: Sunday, Quatorze Juillet.

I have gazed at the tricolour flag floating everywhere on
the island, the flag I have served with honour and loyalty.
My grief is so great that my pen falls from my fingers; there
are feelings that cannot be expressed in words.

380th day.

My little Pierre is now nearly five years old. He is almost
a big boy. I used to wait with impatience for the time to
come when I could take him with me and talk with him;
instruct his young mind, and instil within him the love of
beauty and truth; and thus develop in him so lofty a soul
that the seamy side of life could not defile it. Where are
those dreams now? – and that eternal "Why?"

Dear little Pierre! dear little Jeanne! dear Lucie – how well
I see you in my mind's eye! How the remembrance of you
all gives me the strength to submit to every ill!

MUSIC 7 starts.

Oh – What happy days I used to pass on Sundays, in the midst of my family, playing with my children.

MUSIC 7 ends.

NARRATOR: Reply of the President of the Republic to the petition I addressed to him on October 5, 1895:

"Rejected without comment."

DREYFUS: My blood burns and fever devours me. When will all this end?

MUSIC 8 starts.

How my head throbs! How sweet death would be to me! Oh, my dear Lucie! My poor children! All my dear ones!

What have I done on earth to be doomed to suffer thus?

(DREYFUS begins to lose touch with reality and becomes delirious. His words are paced slowly over the music.)

Yesterday evening I was clapped in irons! Clapped in irons! Shackled!

It is really too much for human shoulders to bear.

Why am I not in the tomb? Oh, everlasting rest!

650th day.

Oh, the ceaseless moaning of the sea. What an echo to my sorrowing soul.

On the horizon I glimpse a wreath of smoke. It must be the mail boat.

No letters. My heart is wounded and torn.

Still no news from my dear ones. The silence of the grave.

What has become of the letters which have been sent to me? Why have they been stopped?

Never any letters.

Strange dreams. Absurd nightmares.

Everything fails me.

My dear little Pierre, my dear little Jeanne, my dear Lucie, all of you, whom I love from the depths of my heart and with all the ardour of my soul, believe me, if these lines reach you, that I have done everything which it is humanly possible to do to stand firm.

If I do not survive, I bequeath my children to France, to my beloved country.

MUSIC 8 ends.

(As LUCIE falls to her knees and clasps her hands in prayer, the music stops.)

LUCIE: Most blessed Father,

Lucie Eugénie Dreyfus, wife of a captain holding a brilliant position in the French Army, of Jewish birth, begs and implores the intervention of the Most Holy Father, Leo XIII.

Alfred Dreyfus, a soldier most devoted to his country, was tried, before a special court-martial, on evidence both false and frivolous, and condemned by his judges to perpetual exile, accompanied by the severest form of punishment.

After the terrible sentence, no one was allowed in the presence of the prisoner who, snatched from the bosom of his family, was transported to Devil's Island, where he endures a wretched existence.

Lucie Eugénie Dreyfus, prostrate at the feet of your Holiness, most humbly supplicates the mercy and compassion of the Father of the Catholic Church. She declares that her husband is innocent, and the victim of a judicial error. Snatched from all association with humankind as he is, this petition is signed by his grief-stricken wife, who, in tears, looks towards the Vicar of

Christ, even as formerly the daughters of Jerusalem turned to Christ Himself.

MUSIC 9 continues.

EPISODE 8

DREYFUS: I must rally all my strength to resist always and yet again I must whisper softly those three words which are my talisman Lucie, Pierre, Jeanne! Lucie, Pierre, Jeanne!

820th day.

I shall struggle against my body, against my brain, against my heart, so long as a shadow of strength is left me. Until they have put me under the ground.

LUCIE: My darling,

There are moments when my heart is so full, when your sufferings re-echo in my soul with such force and so painfully, that I can no longer restrain myself; the separation weighs too heavily on me – it is too cruel; in an outburst of my whole being I stretch out my arms to you. With a supreme effort I strive to reach you. Then I believe myself to be near you, I speak softly of hope and give you courage. All too soon, I am awakened from my dream and brought back sharply to reality by a child's voice, by some noise from without. Then I find myself again alone, so sad, face to face with my thoughts, and especially with the picture of your sufferings. How unhappy you must have been to be deprived of all news. Do not forget, when you receive no letters from me, that I am with you in thought, that I abandon you neither night nor day, and that, if words cannot convey to you the expression of the depths of my love, no obstacle can hinder the union of our hearts and thoughts.

DREYFUS: 910th day.

Shall I still tell you of my affection? It is needless, is it not? For you know it. But what I wish to tell you again is this;

that the other day I re-read all your letters, in order that I might pass some of the too long minutes near a loving heart, and an immense sentiment of wonder arose in me, at this spectacle of your dignity and your courage. If great misfortunes are the touchstone of noble souls, then, oh, my darling, yours is one of the most beautiful and noble souls of which it is possible to dream.

We need misfortune, the sense of the sufferings endured by those for whom we would give our last drop of blood, to understand its force, to grasp its tremendous power. If you knew how often, in the moments of my anguish, I have called to my assistance the thought of you, of our children, to force me to live on, to accept what I should never have accepted but for the thought of duty.

LUCIE: I feel myself wholly incapable of making you share my feelings, since for you, poor exiled one, there is always added to the distress of waiting the ignorance of all that we are doing. Vague sentences, the stringing together of words, give you little more than the assurance of our deep affection and our often-renewed promise that we shall succeed in rehabilitating you.

It breaks my heart not to be able to tell you all that stirs me so deeply and gives me such hope. I suffer from the idea that you are undergoing a martyrdom which, though it must be prolonged physically until the wrong which has been done has been officially admitted, is at least morally useless, and that while I feel more reassured and tranquil, you are passing through periods of anguish and hope that might be spared you.

DREYFUS: 1,000th day.

It is atrocious to suffer thus; yes, all this is appalling, and it is enough to shake every belief in all that makes life noble and beautiful ... but today there can be no consolation for any one of us other than the discovery of the truth, the full light.

My honour is my own possession; it is the patrimony of
our children and it must be restored to them. This honour
I have demanded back from my country. I can only hope
that our harrowing martyrdom may at last come to an end.

LUCIE: I did not succeed in expressing to you in my last letter
and particularly, as I think, in communicating in its full
truth the great confidence we all have, which has grown
even stronger since, in the return of our happiness. I
should like to tell you the joy I feel at seeing the horizon
clearing and at having come nearly to the end of our
sufferings.

If, like me, you could realise the progress we have made
and the distance we have traversed through the depths
of darkness towards the full light, how brightened and
comforted you would feel!

MUSIC 9a.

NARRATOR: Monday, 5th of June, 1899. Instructions from the
Governor to the chief warder:

"Be good enough to let Captain Dreyfus know immediately
of the order of the Court of Appeal. The Court quashes
and annuls the sentence pronounced on December 22,
1894, against Alfred Dreyfus by the first court-martial
of the Military Government of Paris, and orders that the
accused shall be tried before a court-martial at Rennes.

By virtue of this decision, Captain Dreyfus ceases to be
subjected to the convict regimen; he becomes a simple
prisoner under arrest, and is restored to his rank and
allowed to wear his uniform again.

The cruiser S*fax* leaves Port-de-France today, with orders
to take the prisoner from Devil's Island and bring him back
to France.

Communicate to Captain Dreyfus the details of the
decision and the departure of the S*fax*."

DREYFUS: My darling Lucie,

> My heart and soul are with you, with my children, with all of you. I leave Friday. I await with immense joy the moment of supreme happiness to hold you in my arms. A thousand kisses.

LUCIE: Alfred, you are coming home!

MUSIC 9b.

EPISODE 9

NARRATOR: The Court Martial at Rennes.

> *(DREYFUS enters under guard. An old, old man of 39. Five years have passed since his first trial, tortured years on Devil's Island. He has malaria, can hardly walk and his speech is impaired.)*

In the name of the French people!

(DREYFUS tries to stand but cannot.)

Accused. Do you have anything to say?

DREYFUS: I am innocent. I am innocent.

NARRATOR: Is that all?

> Is Captain Dreyfus guilty of having delivered military secrets to a foreign power in order to wage war against France?

(DREYFUS clasps his hands over his ears.)

Guilty Not Guilty Guilty Not Guilty Guilty Guilty Guilty

> The Court declares by a majority of 5 to 2. Yes, the accused is guilty.

Alfred Dreyfus you are sentenced …

(ZOLA interrupts angrily.)

ZOLA: Dreyfus is innocent, that I swear. For this I pledge my
life, for this I pledge my honour.

Before France, before the whole world I swear that
Dreyfus is innocent, and by my forty years of work, by the
authority this labour has given me, I swear that Dreyfus
is innocent. And by all that I have gained, by the name
which I have made for myself, by my work which has
helped to develop French literature, I swear that Dreyfus is
innocent. May all this crumble, may all my work perish if
Dreyfus is not innocent!

He is innocent!

Monsieur le President.

J'Accuse

I accuse!
the Ministers of War,
the courts, the Generals
and their staff and all
who collaborated with them.

I accuse them
of being the diabolical agents
of a judicial error
and defending their deadly work
with revolting cunning.

I accuse them
of being scoundrels
and holding an inquest
of monstrous partiality.

I accuse them
of lying and of fraud
of leading a vile campaign
to mislead the public
and hide their sins.

I accuse them
of violating all human rights
by condemning a man
on testimony kept from him.

I have but one passion
a passion for light
in the name of humanity
that has suffered
and has a right
to happiness.
My burning protest
is the cry of my soul.

NARRATOR: Against his wishes, Dreyfus was granted a Presidential Pardon for a crime he did not commit. He declares:

DREYFUS: The Government of the Republic gives me back my liberty. It is valueless to me without honour. From this day, I shall continue to demand the reparation of the frightful judicial error of which I am still the victim.

I am resolved that all France shall be convinced, by a final judgement, that I am innocent. My heart will not be appeased until there shall be not one Frenchman who imputes to me the abominable crime committed by another.

NARRATOR: Seven years have passed. It is the 20th of July 1906, the Rehabilitation. A guard of honour, crowds and distinguished guests have gathered in the artillery courtyard of the Ecole Militaire in Paris. Dreyfus, raised to the rank of major, arrives in full military uniform.

(DREYFUS stands.)

Vive la France! Vive l'Armée, shout the crowd.

Major Dreyfus, in the name of the President of the Republic, I hereby name you Knight of the Legion d'Honneur.

Vive Dreyfus! Vive Dreyfus!

DREYFUS: Non Messieurs. Vive la France! Vive la Vérité.
Vive la Justice.

MUSIC 10.

EPISODE 10

Epilogue.

NARRATOR: Major Dreyfus with his son Pierre fought valiantly
in World War I. Thereafter, he lived a quiet and withdrawn
life haunted by his memories. The wounds of the shackles
never healed and remained a constant reminder of the
past. Dreyfus died in 1935 and is buried in the cemetery of
Montparnasse in Paris. The second name on his tombstone
is that of his granddaughter Madeleine who was deported
to Auschwitz at the age of 25 where she perished.

The following commentary was pronounced on the
Centenary of the immortal Affair by the grandson of
Dreyfus, Jean-Louis:

DREYFUS: Neither the genocide of 6 million Jews, nor two
world wars have succeeded in obliterating the Dreyfus
Affair with the ashes of forgetfulness.

During 1513 days Dreyfus, isolated on Devil's Island, was
ignorant of the Affair's vicissitudes. How did he survive?
How did he fight against illness, against mental disease,
against the temptation to let himself die?

He had sworn an oath to his wife and children to regain
the honour of his name. Under a burden of unbearable
proportions, he was torn between two images of himself:
the honest soldier he was and 'the vile rascal' he
represented. 'My life belongs to my country, but not my
honour.'

He inherited from Judaism, the indomitable will to survive,
unwilling to break, unwilling to submit.

The Dreyfus Affair – an immortal Affair - remains an example of a power that is deeply rooted in each one of us; the resilience of the human mind, that mysterious fortitude which resists and says No;

NO to force! NO to tyranny! NO to injustice!

MUSIC 11.

Hymne à la Vérité sung.

LUCIE:

Célébrons tous, célébrons ta victoire
Célébrons tous ton triomphe, ô vérité !
Règne seule et que ta gloire éclaire,
Eclaire l'humanité!

LUCIE, DREYFUS, ZOLA:

Règne à jamais règne à jamais,
règne à jamais sur la terre,
Célébrons tous l'humanité
Règne seule, ô verité.

Translation

Let us all celebrate your victory
And rejoice in your triumph, oh truth.
Reign supreme and may your glow
Radiate throughout humanity.

Reign supreme and forever
Forever on this earth,
Let all humanity celebrate
Reign supreme, oh truth.

END

'J'Accuse', as published in *L'Aurore* on 13th January, 1898

La Libre Parole, 'Down with the Jews'. Inset: portrait of Drumont

RAGE AND OUTRAGE

Rage and Outrage (French title *Rage et Outrage*) was first performed on ARTE/Channel 4 in April 1994 with the following cast:

EMILE ZOLA	Jean-Marc Bori
EDOUARD DRUMONT	Lambert Wilson
CHANTEUSE	Ute Lemper

Director, Raoul Sangla
Conductor, Diego Masson
Piano, Jeff Cohen
Music, Songs of the 19th century
Orchestration, Luciano Berio

Sequence 1

THE INNOCENCE OF DREYFUS - I

Piano solo.

Arrival of participants. Author arrives with images and texts. He circles the words 'Rage' and 'Outrage' and hands letter to the chanteuse who reads text aloud. Piano enters at the end of the third paragraph.

Devil's Island, 5 October 1895

Letter from Alfred Dreyfus to the President of the French Republic.

Accused and then condemned on the evidence of handwriting for the most infamous crime a soldier can commit, I have declared and I declare once again that I never wrote the letter with which I was charged and I have never forfeited my honour.

For a year, I have been struggling alone, conscious of my innocence, in the most terrible circumstances which can befall a man. I do not speak of physical suffering, that is nothing, a broken heart is everything.

To suffer by myself is frightful but to know that those dear to me are suffering on my behalf is unbearable.

My whole family is in torment for an abominable crime which I did not commit.

I do not beg for pardon or favours or even assurances. What I ask is that the light of truth should be shed upon the conspiracy which has made victims of my unhappy family and myself.

(CHANTEUSE continues to read silently. Then aloud.)

What gives me strength are the thoughts of Lucie and my children.

Ah; my dearest children! I am not afraid to die. But before dying, I would like to know that your names have been cleansed of this filth.

As piano solo ends, CHANTEUSE reads aloud.

12 January 1896.

Answer from the President of the French Republic.

Rejected, without any comment.

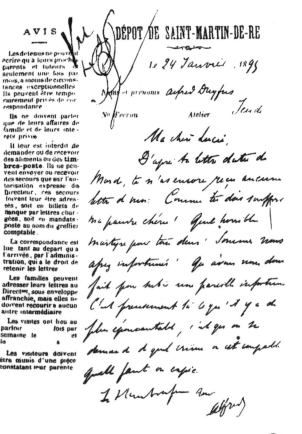

Censored letter to Lucie from the exiled Dreyfus

Sequence 2

THE INNOCENCE OF DREYFUS - II

Voice and accordion.

Original
L'Innocence de Dreyfus

Depuis longtemps un soldat de la France souffre un exilé
accablé de mé-pris pauvre martyre malgré son innocence
fut condamné sans rien avoir compris
en l'accusant de honte et d'infamie
pour épargner des lâches imposteurs
il fut choisi dans leur ignominie
comme victime de bordereau menteur.

(Refrain)

Tu reviendras vaillant martyr de France pauvre exilé banni
de ton pays
souris en fin à ta belle espérance
en maudisant les lâches ennemis.

Dans son erreur toute la France entière
a cru pourtant à ces absurdités
Mais il survint un homme de lumière
Emile Zola disant la vérité
Malgré tous ceux qui lui jettent la pierre
Il a bravé la France avec honneur
Pour ramener aux orphelins le père
Depuis longtemps accablé de douleur.

(Refrain)

Translation
Innocence of Dreyfus

For too many years
A soldier of France
Has suffered alone

A martyr condemned
Abandoned in silence
Shamed and accursed
To save the corrupt
And their cowardly plans.

(Refrain)

One day you'll return, o valiant Frenchman
Wrongly exiled from your native land
The beauty of hope will shine upon you
Your dastardly foes forever banned.

The whole land of France
Bewildered, misled
Was shown the true light
By Zola
Who, braving the stones
Armed only with words
Saved the poor children
Their father.

(Refrain)

Sequence 3

THE INNOCENCE OF DREYFUS - III

Flute, violin, clarinet and cello. Text over music.

DRUMONT: When the French have been stripped to the bone, smothered in the excrement and spittle of Jews, refugees, foreigners, beggars and all other stateless ones who have overrun our unfortunate country, Frenchmen will come looking for me and my comrades.

Then we will cleanse this country, as other great men have done before us.

Sequence 4

THE ANTI-JEWISH MARSEILLAISE

Chorus and orchestra.

ZOLA: The poison is the violent hatred for the Jews which has been fed to the people every morning for years. There is a gang of poisoners, and, hear this, they do it in the name of morality, in the name of Christ, as avengers and dispensers of justice.

Introductory music starts.

ZOLA: In these terrible days of moral strife, at a time when public conscience seems to have darkened, it is to you dear France that I address myself, to the nation, to the homeland.

What has happened beloved France? How is it that your people of good heart and good sense have reached these depths of fear and intolerance?

Original
La Marseillaise Antijuive

Tremblez, youpins, et vous, perfides,
L'opprobre de tous les partis,
Contre nous de la juiverie
Le troupeau hurlant s'est levé *(bis).*

Français, pour nous, ah! quel outrage
D'être insultés par ces bandits,
Balayons donc tous ces youdis
Que notre faiblesse encourage.

Aux armes, antijuifs, formez vos bataillons.
Marchons, marchons,
Qu'un sang impur abreuve nos sillons.

Eh! quoi cette race pourrie
De Dreyfusards, de va-nu-pieds
Insulterait notre Patrie,
Ferait la loi dans nos foyers! *(bis)*
Aux juifs fais mordre la poussière,
Fais rendre gorge à ces voleurs
De notre or et de notre honneur
Puis chasse-les hors la frontière.

Aux armes, antijuifs, formez vos bataillons.
Marchons, marchons,
Qu'un sang impur abreuve nos sillons.

Translation
The Anti-Jewish Marseillaise

Start trembling Yids and traitors
Despised by one and all
If the Jews rise up against us
Avenging hordes will roar *(repeat)*.

Frenchmen it's an outrage
Our weakness has allowed
Let's rid ourselves of outlaws
May Jews be disavowed.

To arms antisemites! Form your battalions!
March on, march on
May our fields be drenched with their tainted blood.

And how this rotten race
Of Dreyfus and the likes
Insult our noble homeland
Dictating all our lives! *(repeat)*
Bite the dust, you Jews, you thieves
We'll drive you from our shores
You will not profit from your vice
Just stay with you and yours.

To arms antisemites! Form your battalions!
March on, march on
May our fields be drenched with their tainted blood.

*CHANTEUSE reads aloud, over musical improvisation, extract of
DREYFUS' letter from Devil's Island to his wife LUCIE.*

Such torment finally passes the bounds of human
endurance. It renews each day the poignancy of the agony.
It crushes an innocent man alive into the tomb.

At times, I am so despairing, so worn out, that I have a
longing to lie down and just let my life ebb away. I cannot
by my own act hasten the end. I have not, I shall never
have that right.

This punishment is beyond endurance.

Sequence 5

FOLKSONG I

Voice and Piano.

Original
Volkslied: **Was i träumt hab'**

Auf ferner, weltverlass'ner Insel
Sitzt ein Gefangener still
und denkt:

Ob jemals mir in diesem Leben
Mein Frankreich wohl die Freiheit schenkt!

Und weiter denkt er seines Weibes,
Das treu um ihren Gatten weint,
Da murmelt er in seinem Kerker,
Den selten nur ein Strahl bescheint:

Weißt du, Frankreich was i träumt hab',
Ich habe in die Zukunft g'sehn.

Ich sab mein Weib wie einen Engel,
Um Rettung und um Freiheit fleh'n
Und du, La France, ließt nicht vergebens
Sie bitten um Gerechtigkeit,
Ich sah mich wieder an der Seine,
Geehrt, wie einst in alter Zeit.

Translation
What I dreamt

Alone on an island
Lost to the world
The lonely prisoner sits.

When will the country of my soul
Accept my innocence?

He tenderly thinks
Of his wife in grief
And murmurs
in his dank dark cell:

Do you know France what I dreamt
One day there came a vision
My beloved, a shining angel
Lighting up my gloomy prison.
She begged for justice and for freedom
And France, at last you heard her
For by the Seine I walked again
As once I did with honour.

Sequence 6

FOLKSONG II

Clarinet and piano.

CHANTEUSE reads extracts of letters from ALFRED DREYFUS on Devil's Island to his wife LUCIE.

December: 13, 1895

They will certainly end by killing me through repeated sufferings or by forcing me to seek in suicide an escape from insanity.

Each night I dream of my wife and children. But what terrible awakenings! When I open my eyes and find myself in this cell, I have a moment of such anguish that I could close my eyes forever, never to see or think again.

Thursday September 3, 1896, 9 o'clock, morning.

The last boat has come and has not brought my letters!

Tuesday September 8, 1896.

My dear little Pierre, my dear little Jeanne, my dear Lucie, – all of you whom I love from the depths of my heart and with all the ardour of my soul – believe me, if these lines reach you, that I have done everything which is humanly possible to hold out.

Sequence 7

THE YID'S POLKA

Chorus and orchestra.

Text read over musical introduction.

DRUMONT: One recognises the Jews thus: the celebrated hooked nose, squinting eyes, clenched teeth, ugly ears and deformed nails, sagging belly, flat feet, rounded knees, the ankle poking outwards, the hands sweaty and limp; these are all signs of the hypocrite and the traitor – they often have one arm shorter than the other.

Original
La Polka des Youpins

V'là qu'danse les rues d'Paris

73

On n'trouve plus qu'des youdis.
A chaque pas sur votre chemin
Vous n'voyez qu'des youpins.
C'est une race de vermine,
Ils ont de tristes mines.
On d'vrait les expulser
Ou bien les assommer.

Tra la la la la
La la la la la
Chassez ces coquins
Oh! les sales youpins.

D'après leurs renseignements
Dreyfus est innocent,
Mais ils sont incapables
D'découvrir le coupable.
On peut l'dire sans vergogne
Ils ont triste besogne,
Quand leur race périra
Alors chacun chantera.

Tra la la la la
La la la la la
Chassez ces coquins
Oh! les sales youpins.

C'est vraiment une sale clique
Qu'ces mangeurs de mastic,
Ils sont fourbes et menteurs,
Orateurs, beaux parleurs,
Ils sont très braves aussi,
Rien que l'jour, pas la nuit,
Mais au premier coup d'feu
Ils s'sauvent à qui mieux mieux.

Tra la la la la
La la la la la

Chassez ces coquins
Oh! les sales youpins.

Ils sont marchands d'assiettes
Ou bien de bicyclettes,
Quoiqu'habitant Paris,
Ce sont des sans-patrie;
Faut chasser cette espèce
A coups d'pied dans les fesses
Chassez tous les youdis!
C'est le cri de Paris.

Tra la la la la
La la la la la
Chassez ces coquins
Oh! les sales youpins.

Translation
The Yid's Polka

Here in the streets of Paris
Only Yids are to be found
At each and every turn
Only Yids are seen around
Such a race of vermin
With their pathetic grins
Should either be thrown out
Or else be done right in.

Tra la la la la
La la la la la
Kick out the dirty Yids
Hip! Hip! Hip! Hurrah!

In their twisted minds
Dreyfus is not to blame
Although the guilty party
Not one of them can name
Their sordid end is nigh

So when their race is gone
We'll celebrate with song
Holding our heads up high.

Tra la la la la
La la la la la
Kick out the dirty Yids
Hip! Hip! Hip! Hurrah!

A really dirty clique
Who speak well and who speak pious
What they eat will make you sick
They're treacherous and liars
Brave by day but not by night
And when a shot is heard,
They run off and they disappear
And vanish out of sight.

Tra la la la la
La la la la la
Kick out these dirty Yids
Hip! Hip! Hip! Hurrah!

Paris lodgers no one wants
Peddling plates and bikes
A good kick up their rotten arse
Should rid us of these kikes
Without a home to call their own
They spread themselves around
Down with the Yids. Down with the Yids
Leave Paris well alone.

Tra la la la la
La la la la la
Kick out the dirty Yids
Hip! Hip! Hip! Hurrah!

Sequence 8

FOLKSONG III

Voice and accordion.

Original
Volkslied: **Was i träumt hab'**

Im Arbeitszimmer, da lehnt Zola,
Des Freundes Schicksal dauert ihn:
Hätt' Flügel er, sie müssten tragen
Ihn dahin, wo die Wolken zieh'n,
Zu Dreyfus, den er wollt' befreien
Von einem feilen Kriegsgericht,
Da über ihn, als wie Erleuchtung
Es kommt und eine Stimme spricht:

Weißt du, Zola, was i träumt hab'
Hab' in die Zukunft eini g'sehn,
Um ihn, den du so sehr beklagtest,
Wird bald der Freiheit Banner weh'n.
Unschuldig hat er viel gelitten,
Doch bald ist seine Prüfung aus
Und Frankreichs stolzeste Fregatte
Geleitet meerwärts ihn nach Haus.

Translation
What I dreamt

Alone in his study
Zola sat pondering
The fate of his friend
Has left him wondering
If Zola had wings he would fly
To free Dreyfus from grief and lie
Suddenly in blinding light
A gentle voice is heard:

Do you know Zola what I dreamt
I looked into the future
The friend for whom you feel such sorrow
Will for sure be freed tomorrow
The test of time is at an end
A proud ship of France is sailing
And once again the flag will fly
To honour his returning.

DRUMONT: No weakness, no pity for the Jews!

Sequence 9

DREYFUS ABOVE ALL I

Orchestra.

ZOLA: I have already said how this barbaric campaign, which takes us back a thousand years, arouses my craving for brotherhood, my passion for tolerance and human equality.

DRUMONT: These are people who have always, under every regime, in every corner of the earth, whether it be in relationship to Muslims or Christians, been the object of the same insults and the same hatreds. How do you explain all that?

ZOLA: To return once again to the wars of religion and persecution – to wish to exterminate one another, race by race is so utterly senseless that, in this century of enlightenment, such a concept is only for imbeciles.

DRUMONT: Yes, our day is coming, but alas in the middle of the storm.

If we were overthrown, every word that we have uttered, every word that evoked the derision of the press would explode with sudden fury and 'The Jews – it is the Jews!' would take on a terrible meaning. For the French once again, the end would justify the means.

ZOLA: And I refuse to believe that such a movement could once again prosper in this country of free thought; brotherly love and clear intellect.

Sequence 10

PRISONER'S LAMENT

Voice and orchestra.

Original
Песнь узника

Невинный я на острове томлюся,
Враги хотят погибели моей!
За честь свою я смерти не страшуся,
Семью мне жаль, страшна разлука с ней!
Тоска и скорбь мне сердце сильно гложут,
Поруган я отчизною своей!
Но правды свет мне друг пролить поможет.
Семью мне жаль, тяжка разлука с ней.
Огонь горит в груди,
Отвагой сердце бьётся,
Отчизну ли свою спасти
Страданье мне даётся?
Пусть все клянут меня,
Меня ли жизнь прельщает?
Судьба моя всего меня
Лишь верой насыщает.

Phonetic Transcription
P'esn'j uznika

Nevinny ya na ostrove toml'yusya
Vragi k'hotiat pogibeli moey
Za tchest'j svoyou ya smerti ne strashoosya
Semyou mn'je zhal'j, strashna razlooka s n'ej
Toska i skorb'j mne serdtse sil'jno gloz'joot
Paroogan ya otchiznoyou svoyey
No pravdy svet mn'je droug prolit'j pomozhet
Sem'you mn'je zhal'j, t'jazhka razlouka s nyey.
Ogon'j gorit v groud'ji
Otvagoy serdtse b'yotsya
Otchiznoo l'i svoyoo spastee
Stradan'jie mn'je daetsya?
Poust'j vs'je klyanoot men'ya
Men'ya l'i zjizn'j prel'jshtchaet?
Sood'jba moya, vsevo men'jya
L'ish v'yeroy nasishchaet.

Translation
Prisoner's Lament

All innocent I suffer on this island
My enemies wish only for my death
Though unafraid to perish for my honour
Grieving for loved ones cannot be endured.
Yearning and sadness devastate my spirit
Honour and trust no longer my birthright
My motherland deserts her faithful soldier
Still I rely on truth to show the light.
Heartsick to be apart
My brain's on fire, my heart courageous
How can this penance redeem my country
My fate a lifetime of oppression.
True faith is my support
Life means no more to me than longing
Despised, rejected, my soul in torment
Branded a traitor to my land.

ZOLA: Dreyfus is innocent, that I swear. For this I pledge my life, for this I pledge my honour.

Before France, before the whole world I swear that Dreyfus is innocent and by my forty years of work, by the authority this labour has given me, I swear that Dreyfus is innocent. And by all that I have gained, by the name which I have made for myself, by my work which has helped to enrich French literature, I swear that Dreyfus is innocent. May all this crumble, may all my work perish if Dreyfus is not innocent!

He is innocent!

Sequence 11

INTERROGATION OF DREYFUS

Voices, strings, two accordions and piano.

Original
L'Interrogatoire de Dreyfus

Accusé, votre nom, votre âge?
Mon colonel, je n'en sais rien!
Vous êt's inculpé d'espionnage
Avec l'Etat-Major Prussien.
Dit's la vérité.
Toute la vérité!

Non, dit Dreyfus impertubable,
Colonel, on vous a trompé
J'vous jur'que je n'suis pas coupable.
Le Rabbin m'a déjà coupe!

Au Ministère de la Guerre,
Quand arriva le bordereau,
Vous étiez officier stagiaire
D'puis qué'qu'temps au deuxièm'bureau;
Dit's la vérité,
Rien qu'la vérité;

81

Mon président, j'suis pas coupable,
Ça, c'est la faute aux généraux
Qui ont dit: Faut prouver, que diable!
Qu'c'est Dreyfus qu'a fait l'bordereau.

On vous a vu, ce n'est pas niable,
Fureter toujours et partout;
Vous vouliez, s'pèce d'misérable,
Renseigner les All'mands sur tout!
Dit's la vérité,
Rien q'la vérité.

Mon colonel, je vais vouz dire:
Je cherchais c'qu'on n'peut pas trouver,
Car c'était, non d'une tirlire,
Un youpin qu'a pas un grand nez.

Vous étiez un trist'personnage.
Coureur de femme et de tripot,
Et rien qu'pour vot'dévergondage
On eut dû vous f...iche à l'hostot.
Dit's la vérité,
Rien q'la vérité.

Mon colonel, malgré ma bille,
Qu'a pas l'air de vous amuser,
J'avais qu'une All'mand' très gentille,
Qui m'app'lait: Sa p'tit crott' sucrée.

Maintenant, la preuve est bien faite,
Vous êt's un officier félon,
Vous avez touché d'la galette,
Comme prix de vot' trahison;
V'là, la vérité,
Tout' la vérité;

Non, dit Dreyfus imperturbable.

Colonel, on vous a trompé
J'vous jur' que je n'suis pas coupable,
Le Rabbin m'a déjà coupé!

La Moral' de cett' triste histoire,
C'est qu'malgré l'argent des vauriens,
Malgré l'Syndicat, la victoire
Ne restera pas aux youpins,
Ces oiseaux d'malheurs,
Traîtres ou voleurs;
Et chacun reprendra confiance,
Quand tous ces sal's juifs parvenus
Seront chassés de notre France
A grands coups de savat's dans l'cul.

Translation
The Interrogation of Dreyfus

Accused, your name, what is your age?
Sir, I do not know
You stand charged with espionage
For the Prussian foe
Tell the truth
The whole truth!

No Sir, says haughty Dreyfus
In fact you've been misled
Where the Rabbi cut me
My honour grew instead.

A document arrived
At the Ministry of War
When you, a Junior Officer
Served in the Intelligence Corps
Tell the truth
The whole truth!
Sir, I am not guilty
The generals are to blame
They said go to the devil

It's they who bear the shame.

We know that you were seen
Ferreting high and low
You wanted, worthless wretch
To aid the German foe
Tell the truth
The whole truth!

Sir, I will now tell you
I looked and searched and chose
Impossible it was to find
An unhooked Jewish nose.

You were a sorry figure
A philanderer and cheat
You should have been disposed of
Leaving us clean and neat
Tell the truth,
Nothing but the truth!

Sir, I swear despite my beak
Which doesn't seem to please you
One day a German girl I took
Who called me her sweet poo-poo...

Such proof will not acquit
An officer and felon
Who had his just rewards
As payment for high treason
That is the truth
The whole truth!

No Sir, says haughty Dreyfus
In fact you've been misled
Where the Rabbi cut me
My honour grew instead.

The moral of this story
I shall now gladly tell
Despite their dirty money
The Yids will go to Hell
These thieves and wicked traitors
These lousy birds of prey
A good kick up their bums
Will make them go away
So dear France, be thankful
Now – let us go and pray.

Sequence 12

DREYFUS ABOVE ALL - II

Clarinet and two accordions.

DRUMONT: The Jew is the most powerful trouble-maker the
world has ever produced and he goes through life joyously
causing harm to Christians. How happy many would be
to unsheath their swords and defend what the Jews defile
– Christ, the Church and our Homeland!

ZOLA: It is a poison. This rabid hatred of the Jews which is fed
to the people every morning in the name of morality, in
the name of Christ. It is a very simple ploy to fan the fires
of antisemitic rage. What a triumph. Is this not the basis
of the dogma to rekindle once again the intolerance of the
Middle Ages to burn the Jews?

Voice, piano and double bass.

Original
Dreyfus über alles

Heil'ger Dreyfus, Unschuldsseele,
Stolz und Stern des ganzen Seins,
Ohne Falsch und ohne Fehler
Ist Dein Herz, so rein wie kein's!
Nie durchdringt ja Deine Kehle

Daß nichts Unreines sich stehle
Nur ein Bissen Fleisch des Schwein's,
In ein Herz, so rein wie Dein's!

Zola steh' Dir treu zur Seite
Mit Reklameschmiererei'n,
Um des Erdballs Läng' und Breite
Gründlich noch zu seifen ein!
Bis in Abram's Schoß geleite
Er Dich einst aus Not und Pein,
Und des Universums Weite
Mög' dann Euer Spucknapf sein!

Translation
Dreyfus above all

Holy Dreyfus, innocent heart
Our pride and joy forever
Truthful always, never false
Purity is your endeavour
Your soul sustains a life so fine
No lying and no error
Pig-meat does not pass your lips
The thought fills you with terror.

Let Zola stand close by your side
While all the world observes
To cheat the good and simple folk
His famous words he serves
To Abraham he'll shepherd you
And help relieve your sufferance
The universe is large enough to
hear each filthy utterance.

ZOLA: It is a crime to accuse of agitation those,
    who wish France to be generous
    It is a crime to poison the young and the simple
    It is a crime to exploit patriotism for deeds of hatred
    It is a crime ... a crime ... a crime ...

Sequence 13

DOWN WITH THE JEWS

Chorus and percussion.

Original
A bas les juifs

Français, arrachons notre France
Aux Juifs perfides et maudits.
Jurons-le plus de tolérance
Pour cette race de bandits.
Pour défendre notre patrie
Partout formons des bataillons.
Pour terraser la Juiverie
Devenons tous comme de lions.
Pour terraser la Juiverie
Devenons tous comme de lions.

Nous gémissons dans l'esclavage
Des traîtres et des imposteurs,
secouons le honteux servage
de ces youpins faux et menteurs.
Allons braves antisémites,
Trop longtemps ils furent nos rois,
Leurs audaces sont sans limites
Il faut reconquérir nos droits.

Translation
Down with the Jews

Frenchmen let us rescue France
From these accursed Jews
Tolerance we'll show them not
Nor give them strength anew
To save our country from their grasp
A fighting band will form
A pride of lions we'll become
And ban them from these shores
A pride of lions we'll become
And ban them from these shores

We tremble in the slavery
Of traitors and of cheats
Save us from this servitude
Imposed by lying Yids
March on brave antisemites
They've ruled us far too long
Their arrogance is limitless
Our lands win back and hold.

DRUMONT: Listen to the cry emanating from all the corners of France 'Down with the Jews!' Certainly it is a cry from the past, but it is also a cry of the future, for whenever man suffers the same pain he utters the same cry ...

ZOLA: There is no deed more heroic than that of the struggle for truth and justice.
There is nothing greater or more noble.

DRUMONT: The demonstrations taking place all over France to the shouts of 'Down with the Jews!' are, however, very significant. They express quite clearly what the country wants.

ZOLA: By which morality, by which G-d are we guided?

DRUMONT: The impudence, the detestable mad impudence of this race so sure it has conquered France.

ZOLA: It is antisemitism we have to thank for the whole of this lamentable affair.
It was this alone which made the judicial error possible.
It is this alone, which today, drives the crowds insane.

DRUMONT: Death to the Jews!
The cry was uttered at the same time, with the same force, with the same ardour and with the same sincerity as before and, once again, without urging.

ZOLA: Forbidden to speak! The shameful terror reigns, the bravest amongst us are becoming cowards. No-one dares to say any more what he thinks, for fear of being denounced as a traitor.

DRUMONT: I drink to the Republic, to the French Republic which will rid you of these Jews! I drink to France, for to cry 'Long live France!' is to cry 'Down with the Jews!' as France is dying from the Jews.

Long live the Republic!

Down with the Jews!

Lambert Wilson as Drumont from the
ARTE/Channel 4 production of *Rage and Outrage*
Photo: Artial Ltd London

Sequence 14

CODA

Chorus and orchestra.

During the Coda, the CHANTEUSE reads extracts from letters of DREYFUS from Devil's Island.

Violent palpitations of the heart this morning. I am suffocating. The machine struggles on. How much longer can this last? Terrible heat. The hours are like lead.

This must end.

Ah! Humanity.

Ah! My beloved children.

DRUMONT: *(With percussion.)* The Jews have to be eternally blind as they have always been not to realise what is awaiting them. They will be taken away as scrap and the people that they oppress so harshly, that they exploit with such ferocity, will dance with joy when they learn that justice has been done.

The leader who will suddenly emerge incarnating the idea of an entire nation will do whatever pleases him. He will have the right of life and death; he will be able to employ any means that suit his purpose.

We will ask him to satisfy what is in the hearts of all of us, the need for justice, and to punish those who deserve it.

The great organiser who will unite the resentments, anger and suffering, will achieve a result which will resound through the universe. He will return to Europe its prestige for 200 years.

Who is to say that he is not already at work?

Sequence 15

FINALE

Departure of participants.

CHANTEUSE approaches the painter, takes the brush and begins to paint. She points to the graffiti and asks the painter.

'Is that the Dreyfus Affair?'

The painter is irritated.

'No. I'll show you, what is the Dreyfus Affair!'

and kicks the bucket of paint at the wall. It is red paint. As it runs down the wall and the participants begin to depart:

ZOLA: Young antisemites. Do they really exist? So there are young minds, young souls which have already been infected by this poison. What sorrow! What trepidation for the approaching twentieth century!

One hundred years after the Declaration of the Rights of Man, one hundred years after the supreme act of tolerance and emancipation, we are returning to the wars of religion, to the most hideous and absurd fanaticism!

And somehow we can understand this among certain men who play a role, who have an image to uphold and a voracious ambition to satisfy.

But amongst the young? Amongst those who are born and who are growing up with the blossoming of rights and freedom which we dreamt would illuminate the forth-coming century?

They are the awaited work force and are already self-declared antisemites. They wish to open the new century by massacring all the Jewish citizens, simply because they are of a different race and of a different faith!

The city of equality and fraternity! If our youth really came to this, we would have to weep and deny all hope for human happiness.

Oh Youth! Youth! I beg you consider the great task which awaits you. You are the architects of the future. You are the ones who will lay the foundations of the century to come which we profoundly believe will resolve the problems of the past.

Youth! Youth! Remember the suffering which your fathers endured. Those terrible battles they had to fight in order to gain the freedom in which you rejoice today.

You were not born under tyranny. You do not know what it is to awake each morning with the heel of a boot on your breast. You did not fight to escape the sword of a dictator or bear the crushing weight of a dishonest judge. Thank your fathers. Do not commit the crime of applauding lies, to campaign with brute force for the intolerance of fanatics and the greed of the ambitious. Dictatorship is the result.

Youth! Youth! Remain always on the side of justice. If the concept of justice were to fade within your soul, you will be open to grave dangers.

Youth! Youth! Be humane. Be generous. Even if we are wrong, stay with us when we say that an innocent is suffering unbearable pain and that our outraged and anguished hearts are breaking.

How can you not dream a dream of chivalry if somewhere a martyr succumbs to hatred without coming to his aid? Who, if not you, will undertake the sublime task of launching himself into this dangerous and superb cause and take the lead in the name of true justice?

Where are you heading, young people? Where are you heading you students fighting in the streets, demonstrating, casting the passions and hopes of your twenty years into the midst of our troubles?

We are heading towards humanity, truth and justice.

The lights are lowered as the participants depart but one of them returns – he has left his coat behind. He notices a swastika which has been sprayed over the painted blood – he ignores it and leaves.

END

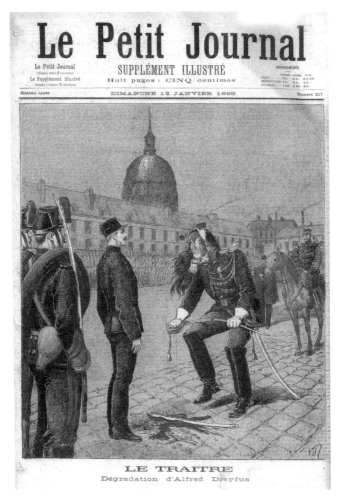

The degradation ceremony of Captain Dreyfus,
in the courtyard of the Ecole Militaire in Paris, 1895

Dreyfus averring his innocence. *The Graphic London*, 1899

THE DREYFUS AFFAIR

The Dreyfus Affair (German title *Dreyfus – Die Affäre*) was first performed at Deutsche Oper Berlin on 8th May 1994 with the following cast:

ALFRED DREYFUS	Paul Frey
LUCIE DREYFUS	Aimee Willis
MATHIEU DREYFUS	Hagen Henning
EMILE ZOLA	Artur Korn
WALSIN ESTERHAZY	Peter Edelmann
MARIE	Hermine May
EDOUARD DRUMONT	David Griffith
COL. SCHWARTZKOPPEN	Otto Heuer
GEN. BOISDEFFRE	Ivan Sardi
GEN. GONSE	Clement Bieber

Director, Torsten Fischer
Conductor, Christopher Keene
Stage design/costumes, Andreas Reinhardt
Music, Jost Meier

Act I

Courtyard of the Ecole Militaire, Paris. Cold winter morning. Sharp wind. Occasional sun. Light snow. Troops line the square. Assembly includes DREYFUS's fellow Officers, veterans, diplomats, etc. Outside the railings the Press and a vast unruly crowd. Whistling, booing and jeering. GENERAL DARRAS on horseback in the centre of the square. Staff officers behind him.

CROWD: Bloody Jew. Filthy Jew. Death to the Traitor! Death to the Traitor!

Death to the Jew, the Filthy Jew, the Traitor. Death to the Filthy Jew.

Death to the Traitor, Death to the Jew. Death. Bloody Jew.

Silence descends on the square. DREYFUS appears escorted by a sergeant-major and 4 gunners. He enters, tries to walk proudly, stumbles and recovers. He is marched in front of GENERAL DARRAS where he stands to attention. His escorts retire 4 paces. DARRAS glares down at DREYFUS. He raises himself in his stirrups and holds his sword high.

GENERAL DARRAS: Alfred Dreyfus. You have been found guilty of the crime of High Treason and sentenced to perpetual deportation and to military degradation. You are no longer worthy to bear arms. In the name of the French people we degrade you.

DREYFUS: Soldiers. An innocent man is being degraded. Vive la France. Vive l'Armée.

CROWD: Bloody Jew. Filthy Jew. Death to the Traitor. Kill the bloody Jew.

Bloody Jew. Filthy Jew. Death to the Traitor. Death to the Jew. Death.

The giant figure of sergeant-major BOUXIN approaches the condemned man. Brutally he rips the decorations from DREYFUS's cap and sleeves, the red stripes from his trousers, his epaulettes and all the insignia of his rank. He casts it all on the ground. He takes DREYFUS's sabre and scabbard and shatters them over his knee.

DREYFUS: I am innocent. I swear on the heads of my wife and children. I am innocent.

CROWD: Bastard. Yid. Traitor. Pig!

Death to the Jew. Bastard. Death to the Traitor. Death to the bloody Jew.

DREYFUS: I am innocent.

DREYFUS is now a tattered figure. He is paraded in front of the troops and his fellow officers. He passes the VETERANS.

VETERANS: Silence. Bastard. Filthy Jew. Traitor. Dirty Pig.

DREYFUS: I am innocent. Vive la France. Vive l'Armee.

CROWD: Death to the Traitor. The filthy Jew. Bastard. Jewish Traitor.

Death to the Jew. The bastard. Death to the Traitor.

DREYFUS: You have no right to insult me. I am innocent.

CROWD: Death to the Traitor. Bastard! Judas! Filthy Yid! Boo! Bastard! Judas! Filthy Yid! Boo! Death to the Traitor. Death to the Traitor!

DREYFUS: I am innocent. I am innocent. Innocent.

CROWD: Boo! Bastard. Judas. Beat the filthy pig to death. Traitor. Bastard, Judas. Death to the Traitor.

DREYFUS: Innocent. .. in ... innocent.

CROWD: Death to the Jews! Death to the Jews!

At the end of the courtyard two Gendarmes seize DREYFUS, handcuff him and haul him into a prison van. The crowd has become hysterical. The military band strikes up the march 'Sambre et Meuse'. Cheering, howling, whistling.

MATHIEU and LUCIE visit DREYFUS in Prison. They do not know but it is the last time they will see him for 5 years. The prisoner is separated from the visitors by double bars. The PRISON DIRECTOR is always present. MATHIEU and LUCIE arrive and wait in the corridor. As they hear the clatter of prison keys and the doors, LUCIE shudders.

LUCIE: I want to kiss Alfred, ask if I may.

MATHIEU: *(Approaching the PRISON DIRECTOR.)* His wife would like to kiss her husband. His wife Lucie seeks your permission to kiss her husband.

PRISON DIRECTOR: No, no. It is not allowed.

MATHIEU: But just think they may be parted for ever.

PRISON DIRECTOR: No!

MATHIEU exits. LUCIE goes up to him anxiously.

LUCIE: May I?

MATHIEU: No. It is not allowed.

LUCIE enters the Prison area. ALFRED is looking at the small photograph of LUCIE and his children. ALFRED and LUCIE stand silently for a moment, lost and embarrassed in front of the PRISON DIRECTOR.

DREYFUS: A blind anger invades my heart when I think of our little ones suffering through their father. What am I doing here? Is it an hallucination? Then I look at my tattered clothes and I know it is reality. Even the convicts around me are worth more than a traitor. At least they killed for jealousy or revenge. My bitterness is great. My heart is torn and bleeding. But I will fight to my dying breath. I only have one aim in life, to find the guilty one.

LUCIE: Only courage my darling, courage. One day you will see your children again. Promise me you will live. Without you I cannot exist. I cannot exist without you.

DREYFUS: Do not weep my darling, do not weep. Fix your gaze ahead of you. Move the hearts of other wives and mothers. Cry out my innocence. Cry it, cry it from the rooftops so that the walls will shake. Cry it out.

LUCIE: I implore you bear your torment bravely. I share your sorrow, the suffering and the shame. I will fight until the whole world recognizes your innocence.

DREYFUS: I feel your heart beating so close to mine. So close, so close. I have loved you so deeply, always. I have loved you from the bottom of my heart.

LUCIE/DREYFUS: The thought of you and our children will give me strength.

LUCIE: *(Approaching the PRISON DIRECTOR.)* May I hold his hand?

PRISON DIRECTOR: No, it is not allowed. Time is up.

DREYFUS: *(Lost in his thoughts.)* One day in our dear France there will arise a man honest and courageous enough to seek and discover the truth.

ALFRED: My darling, until tomorrow. Lucie, until tomorrow.

LUCIE: My darling, until tomorrow Alfred.

They reach out to each other, but cannot touch. LUCIE departs then stops and remains standing deep in her thoughts. She overhears in the background.

PRISON DIRECTOR: Strip him! Search him! Clap him in irons. He leaves for Devil's Island tonight.

LUCIE rushes back but the iron doors are slammed in her face. She collapses in horror in MATHIEU's arms.

Night falls. INTERLUDE. The journey to Devil's Island.

Devil's Island. DREYFUS alone in his cell. It is night. Guards outside. The tricolore. A guard flashes a light in his face through the cell window. DREYFUS awakes with a start.

DREYFUS: My brain reels and my blood burns. Fever devours me. When will all this end? Silence. Eternal silence. Never a human voice. I am alone.

In the scenes which follow, DREYFUS remembers or dreams of episodes in his life. These are re-enacted on stage and, simultaneously, he reacts to his memories on Devil's Island.

DREYFUS falls back in his bunk. He dreams of the Synagogue when he was a boy during the Franco-Prussian War. He remembers the service and the sound of the approaching German army.

CONGREGATION: *(Hebrew)* Adaushem Echod. *[The Lord is One.]*

CANTOR 1: Shema Yisroel Adaushem Elaukenu Adaushem Echod. Echod. *[Hear Oh Israel, The Lord our G-d, The Lord is One. One.]*

CANTOR 2: Shema Yisroel Adaushem Elaukenu Adaushem Echod. *[Hear Oh Israel, The Lord our G-d, The Lord is One.]*

CANTOR 3: Shema Yisroel Adaushem Echod. *[Hear Oh Israel, The Lord is One.]*

RABBI: Eternal God, Lord of the Universe, from your Holy dwelling place bless and protect the French people. I beseech the God of Israel to imbue the Ministers of France with the spirit of goodwill for the children of Israel.

CANTOR 1: Ovinu Malkenu chosvenu besefer chajim tauvim Ovinu Ovinu Malkenu batel machschwaus saunenu Ovinu Malkenu Ovinu Ovinu Malkenu kera roah gezar dinenu. *[Our Father, Our King, seal us in the book of happy life, Our Father, Our Father, Our King, annul the designs of those who hate us. Our Father, Our King, repeal the evil sentence of our judgement.]*

CONGREGATION: *(Bass voices)* Shema yisroel Adaushem Elaukenu Adaushem Echod. *[Hear Oh Israel, The Lord our G-d, The Lord is One.]*

CANTOR 2/3: Echod. *[One.]*

RABBI: In this great country of France whose flag is a glorious and immortal symbol of Justice, Brotherhood and Liberty, we, the sons of Israel have become equals.

LUCIE: *(From afar.)* Alfred is innocent, innocent, innocent. Vive la France. Vive l'Armée.

DREYFUS: Vive la France. Vive l'Armée.

RABBI: May France at this time of conflict be strong and victorious. Long live France. France and her Army.

CONGREGATION: Long live France, France and her Army.

The voice of DREYFUS as a boy (tape) is heard.

THE BOY DREYFUS: Papa, when I grow up, I want to be a soldier.

DREYFUS dreams of his passing out parade. Marching cadets are seen and heard.

CADETS: Honour and Glory the Class of Eighty Two. Honour and Glory to the officer cadets. Liberté, Egalité, Fraternité. Vive la France, Vive l'Armée.

The CADETS receive their accolades. So does DREYFUS. (Fellow cadets gaze at him suspiciously.)

DREYFUS wakes from his sleep. He thinks of LUCIE.

DREYFUS: Lucie, my thoughts are with you. You are my strength. I must live. I must prove my innocence.

On one part of the stage the German Embassy in Paris comes into view. Schwartzkoppen is in his office with Esterhazy. Madame Bastian is hiding in the corridor.

ESTERHAZY: The material is important. It is worth a high price. This 'Bordereau' contains valuable information. I will be back with more.

ESTERHAZY hands the documents to SCHWARTZKOPPEN, who hands him money in return.

DREYFUS: If I would only know who the guilty one is. I must find out. I must find out. I have to find out. I am innocent, innocent, innocent.

ESTERHAZY: *(With false pathos.)* It is contemptible to betray one's Fatherland, but I have no other choice. It is for my wife and my children. I must save them from poverty and ruin. I cannot say more.

After ESTERHAZY leaves, SCHWARTZKOPPEN studies the 'Bordereau', he tears it up and throws it into the wastepaper basket. He leaves his office. MADAME BASTIAN empties the basket into her apron. She hands its content to Commandant HENRY, who comes to make his regular collection.

On Devils' Island, DREYFUS dreams of the intimate family atmosphere at home. He hears LUCIE playing the piano. MATHIEU, PIERRE and JEANNE are there. The office of MERCIER comes slowly into view.

DREYFUS: *(Island)* My dear Pierre, my little Jeanne, darling Lucie, I love you all from the depth of my heart. I love you with all my heart. I cannot say more.

LUCIE: *(At home, sings a lullaby to her children.)* In the Holy Temple, in the corner, sits the mother Bat-Zion alone.

DREYFUS: *(Island)* Aaaaaaaaa.

MERCIER: *(In his office)* This must cease. Military secrets passing into the hands of the enemy. Traitors in the Army. My career is at stake.

LUCIE: *(At home)* Sits the mother Bat-Zion alone
Her two sweet children she rocks with love
and sings them to sleep with a lullaby

DREYFUS: *(Island)* Aaaaaaaa.

MERCIER: *(Office)* What is the bureau doing? Sleeping?

HENRY: *(Office)* Minister. More evidence has come to light. It is a 'Bordereau', military secrets. We have gone through the listing of officers on the general staff. We have marked the suspicious one.

LUCIE: *(At home)* Under the children's cradle sits a snow white kid.

PIERRE: *(At home)* Cradle, kid.

JEANNE: *(At home)* Cradle, kid.

LUCIE/PIERRE/JEANNE: *(At home)* The kid, destined to wander. Will this be your fate? Raisins and Almonds. Raisins... and... Almonds. Sleep... my little ones... sleep.

DREYFUS: *(Island)* Aaaaaaaaaaaa.

MERCIER: *(Office)* Yes, of course, a Jew. A Jew from the Alsace, Alfred Dreyfus. Of course he is the guilty one.

HENRY: *(Office)* We have compared the handwriting. Here they are.

MERCIER: *(Office)* They look similar. Test his handwriting. Interrogate him. Make him confess. Prepare the order for his arrest.

LUCIE: *(At home)* Sleep now, my little ones, sleep.

MERCIER: *(Office)* It is to be kept secret. *(As he is leaving.)* Lose no time.

DREYFUS: *(Island)* Aaaaaaaaaa ... Cradle, kid, children, children, little ones... sleep.

DREYFUS dreams of his arrest at headquarters. Present: DU PATY, GRIBELIN and others. HENRY is behind the curtain. DU PATY wears a black glove over his right hand. DREYFUS only appears to be present.

DU PATY: Complete this inspection form. I have a letter to write to the General. I have hurt my finger. Could you write it for me? *(Dictates a prepared text.)* Having to retrieve the documents I passed to you before my departure on manoeuvres. Please return them urgently. They concern firstly a note on the hydraulic brake of the 120 Cannon. *(DU PATY interrupts his dictation.)* What is wrong with you Captain? You are trembling. Are your fingers cold? Be careful. This is serious. *(Continuing the dictation.)* Secondly, a note concerning the covering troops. Thirdly, a note on Madagascar. *(DU PATY puts his hand on DREYFUS's shoulder.)* Dreyfus, in the name of the law I arrest you. You are accused of High Treason.

DREYFUS: *(Island)* I... I ... I don't understand, I, I protest, I protest.

DU PATY picks up a copy of the Penal Code, revealing a revolver.

DU PATY: Whoever has conspired or is in contact with the intelligence service of a foreign power shall be punished by death.

DREYFUS: *(Island)* I have never had such contacts, I love my homeland, I am incapable of betrayal. I am the victim of a frightful plot.

DU PATY: By death, shall be punished by death. The evidence is overwhelming. Overwhelming.

The office at headquarters is faded out.

DREYFUS feverish on the Island. He remembers the scene in the Prison Cell after his arrest. DU PATY arrives carrying a box containing fragments of handwriting.

DREYFUS: Is that box Du Paty's? Am I to identify handwritings? This is mine. This I do not know. And this? I do not know. This is mine, and this one I do not know, mine, do not know, mine, yours, his, mine, not mine, mine, not mine, mine, not mine, mine, not mine...

DREYFUS collapses. He is startled by the sound of DU PATY's voice. DREYFUS follows the orders of DU PATY on the Island like a madman.

DU PATY: *(Behind the stage)* Write standing up 'manoeuvre'. Now sit down and write it. Write it again. Now crouch on the floor, write 'I am', hunch over the bed and write 'leaving on manoeuvres'. Now put on this glove and write it, and now lie on the floor and write it.

DREYFUS remains lying on the floor. (Island)

DU PATY: *(Backstage)* I will come back at night when he is asleep. I will flash a light in his face. Perhaps he will utter a guilty phrase.

Dreyfus tries to raise himself. (Island)

DREYFUS: My sole crime is that I was born a Jew.

DREYFUS on the island remembers the military courtroom where he was tried. Large figure of Christ on the wall. Present: 7 judges (including the Presiding JUDGE) - all army officers, guards, HENRY, handwriting experts and PICQUART. The text of the oath is heard

(Chorus - male voices)

I swear by Almighty God, to speak the truth, the whole truth and nothing but the truth.

JUDGE: Commandant Henry?

HENRY: A person of honour warned me that an officer in the Ministry is a traitor. *(He points to the fictitious figure of DREY-FUS in the dock.)* This man is the traitor. *(DREYFUS reacts furiously on the Island.)* I am not naming the informer. These are military secrets.

JUDGE: *(Presiding.)* Do you state on your honour that the treacherous officer mentioned is Captain Dreyfus?

HENRY: *(Raising his hand to the cross on the wall.)* I swear it!

JUDGE: Captain Alfred Dreyfus, do you have anything to say? No. Then the judges shall retire to consider their verdict.

The Courtroom clears. The judges deliberate alone. During their deliberations DU PATY arrives with a Secret Dossier. He hands it to the judges. DU PATY withdraws. The Courtroom reassembles. Each judge gives his verdict as he looks at the Dossier.

OFFICER: Present Arms! *(A terrible silence. All the Judges raise their hands to their caps in military salute.)*

JUDGE: *(Presiding.)* In the name of the French people! Is Alfred Dreyfus, Captain in the Artillery, guilty of having dealings with a foreign power to the detriment of the Nation?

JUDGES 1-7: *(Individually.)* Guilty! Guilty! Guilty! Guilty! Guilty! Guilty! Guilty!

JUDGES: *(Together.)* Guilty!

DREYFUS: *(Remembers the degradation with horror.)* Innocent man degraded. *(He hears the insults of the crowd.)*

CROWD: Dreyfus, hahaha, hahaha, Captain, guilty, haha. Death to the Traitor. Death to the Jews.

Filthy Jew. Bloody Jew. Death to the Traitor.

LUCIE alone in her temporary home. Three years have passed. In her desperation she addresses a supplication to the Pope.

LUCIE: Holy... Holy Father!

I, Lucie Dreyfus, prostrate at the feet of your Holiness most humbly supplicate the mercy and compassion of the Father of the Catholic Church. I declare that my husband Alfred, Captain in the French Army of Jewish descent, is innocent, innocent. He is the victim of a judicial error. As he is severed from all contact with humankind, this petition is signed by his grief-stricken wife, who in tears looks towards the Vicar of Christ, as formerly the daughter of Jerusalem turned to Christ himself.

LUCIE is joined by PIERRE, JEANNE and friends, amongst them ZOLA.

LUCIE: Monsieur Zola, I have told you everything. We are desperate. Three years have passed. We are at the bottom of an abyss. I have even addressed a petition to his

Holiness the Pope. If we do not find the truth, if he dies there, what will happen to his children?

ZOLA: Madame, I feel for your anguish.

MATHIEU: *(Enters. Excited.)* Monsieur Zola, although I am watched, followed and threatened, I have distributed several thousand copies of the Bordereau throughout Paris, in the hope that someone will recognise the handwriting, but nothing. At long last a banker here has recognised the handwriting of one of his clients. It is that of Count Ferdinand Walsin Esterhazy, a Major in the Infantry. I must pass this information immediately to the Ministry of War.

(MATHIEU leaves.)

ZOLA: The Truth is on the march, the truth, the truth. I feel a great injustice has been committed, I will support your cause.

LUCIE, PIERRE, JEANNE and friends are faded away. Concentration on ZOLA.

ZOLA: What is more simple, what is more natural, than to expose the truth? *(He becomes lost in his thoughts.)* Honest folk, I challenge you, read it and know it. Your hearts will pound with anger and revolt when you think of that fearful suffering on Devil's Island. It is my duty to speak as I will not conspire to abet a crime. My nights would be haunted by the spectre of an innocent, his frightful torture for a crime he did not commit. A hidden poison has led us to delirium. Hatred of the Jews. There lies the guilt. The daily ritual, recited year in year out, in the name of morality, in the name of Christ. Now fresh minds, infected by this poison, greet a new century declaring they will massacre all the Jews, for they are of another race, another faith.

The office of General GONSE. Present: BOISDEFFRE, HENRY, DU PATY and GRIBELIN. PICQUART is facing the General. He carries a batch of documents.

PICQUART: My investigations show that the Court Martial made a mistake.

ZOLA: *(His voice)* ... next century...

PICQUART: I have copies of Esterhazy's handwriting and have compared them with the 'Bordereau'. They are identical.

ZOLA: *(Voice)* ... Jews ... massacred ...

PICQUART: Esterhazy should be brought to this office to give an explanation about the 'Bordereau'.

ZOLA: ... from a different race... of another faith… another… another.

GONSE: Out of the question Picquart. You are lacking balance in this matter. *(Friendly.)* Why are you so interested in establishing the innocence of Dreyfus? What is it to you, if this Jew is on Devil's Island?

PICQUART: But if he is innocent?

GONSE: If you say nothing, no one will know.

PICQUART: My General, what you say is despicable. The evidence against Esterhazy is clear. And as for this secret Dossier. *(Throws the Dossier on the table.)* It contains not one piece of evidence against Dreyfus.

GONSE: Picquart, you are only concerned with your obsession. You are neglecting your duties. You are too preoccupied. I will remove you from your post and send you to the Tunisian front.

PICQUART: I do not know what I am going to do, but I will not take this secret to the grave with me. *(He picks up his papers and the secret Dossier. He begins to leave. BOISDEFFRE beckons to HENRY to retrieve the documents from him.)*

HENRY: Colonel, the General wishes you to leave the Dossier and all other papers here. *(PICQUART returns to his office.)*

The following 4 scenes are shown simultaneously. GONSE in his office (a) with others and later with MERCIER; DU PATY in his office (b) with GRIBELIN; PICQUART alone in his office (c); HENRY alone in his office (d). Later DREYFUS on Devil's Island. The action and texts overlap.

GONSE: *(To DU PATY and GRIBELIN in a)* You must warn Esterhazy of Du Paty's enquiries. But he must not know that the warning comes from us. *(DU PATY returns to his office with GRIBELIN.)*

GONSE: *(To Henry in a)* We need new evidence. We need decisive evidence. Evidence which implicates Dreyfus beyond any doubt.

DU PATY: *(To GRIBELIN in b)* We will send Esterhazy an anonymous letter to warn him. We will sign it 'Esperance'. Then I want you to visit him.

HENRY: *(To GONSE in a)* If I may advise, Picquart should be removed from Paris as quickly as possible.

GONSE: *(To HENRY in a)* I intend to name you Chief of the Department when I have re-posted him. *(HENRY leaves office [a] and enters office d.)*

PICQUART: *(Alone in his office in c)* Fate has chosen me to discover the truth.

GRIBELIN: *(In b)* Where do I find Esterhazy?

HENRY is in his office (d) alone. He is falsifying documents, exchanging signatures, re-arranging and re-gluing words in different ways.

PICQUART: *(In c)* An innocent trembles in jail.

DU PATY: *(In b)* He keeps a whore in Rue Douai. Her name is Madame Pays. He is usually there.

PICQUART: *(In c)* The Traitor is walking free.

HENRY: *(In d) (Looks at his forgery. He is pleased.)* Good... very good … I must congratulate myself.

DREYFUS: *(Island)* Suffocation.

DU PATY: *(In b)* The secret meeting should be at Parc Montsouris, at the public urinals.

DREYFUS: *(Island)* ... Air...

HENRY: *(In d)* Really masterly.

PICQUART: *(In c)* What may have been an error, could become a crime.

DREYFUS: *(Island)* It is unbearably hot.

BOISDEFFRE: *(To Gonse in a)* Contact General Mercier immediately and ask him to come here.

HENRY: *(In d)* Good... very good. This should be sufficient.

BOISDEFFRE: *(In a)* He must inspect the secret Dossier.

DREYFUS: *(Island)* Fever...

PICQUART: *(In c)* A crime, what a tragedy for France, for France, for France.

MERCIER arrives in office (a) he is furious. He takes the Secret Dossier from GONSE, opens it and begins to search. He pulls out a document, lights a match and burns it.

DREYFUS: *(Island)* Delirium...

MERCIER leaves (a). GONSE puts the Dossier in his desk. HENRY enters and hands him his forgery. GONSE studies it. He inserts it into the Secret Dossier which he then hands to HENRY. Light goes out in the office.

DREYFUS in his cell on Devil's Island. In one hand he holds his family photograph. He kisses it. He is almost unrecognisable, a pathetic figure disintegrating physically and spiritually. His ankles are bandaged with bload soaked rags. His small window has been mostly boarded up. Temperature and humidity are unbearable. Mosquitos and insects infect his cell. He fears his end is near. He stands by the window gasping for air.

DREYFUS: *(Island)* Trembling... strange images... Delirium. It is too much. It cannot last much longer. I am so weary, everything is black. My heart is overwrought, my heart, my heart, my brain is destroyed. I cannot gather my thoughts. … my my ... I cannot my thou… thoughts... not... gather... together... Lucie my darling... my beloved children... oh I love you all, all. Love... torture... fever... torment... love... anger... aah...

Jailers enter carrying irons. They shackle DREYFUS to his bed. DREYFUS falls into an hallucinatory state. He sees himself in his coffin, immobile (as in the cell). The Cross at the Court Martial becomes visible on which he sees himself crucified. Standing by the Cross is a General (MERCIER but unrecognised by DREYFUS) drawing a sword (Degradation).

ESTERHAZY: *(Not recognisable, voice distorted.)* Haha hahaha ha ha ...

LUCIE, MATHIEU, PIERRE and JEANNE are on the stage. They are in a maze. DREYFUS stretches his arms towards LUCIE (Parting) but cannot reach her. The Generals arrive (Trial and Degradation). DREYFUS beckons for their help, but they ignore him. LUCIE is now running, when she finally reaches the iron gates they slam in front of her (Parting).

ESTERHAZY: Hahahahah ha ha hahaha ... *(His hysterical and satirical laughter is drowned by the Orchestra.)*

ACT II

Gaiety and revelry in the Moulin Rouge. Gambling room and chambre privee. An enormous crowd with celebrities, officers, etc. Music and dancing. A wild Can-Can is in progress. Marguerite (MARIE) Pays, ESTERHAZY's mistress and former prostitute, moves amongst the crowd and approaches the stage. She is attractive and flirtatious.

CROWD: We want Marie, Marie give us a song!

　　We want Marie, a soldier's song!

MARIE: I was sad and I was lonely
　　Nameless men took pleasure from me
　　When passions rose, their pockets jingled
　　When passion waned, their handouts dwindled.

CROWD: Poor Marie. Poor Marie.

MARIE: When passions waned, their handouts dwindled.
　　Then, one day, the bugle sounded
　　And, in one fell swoop, he mounted
　　Sabre held high in his hand.

CROWD: Bravo Marie. Bravo Marie
　　Sabre held high in his hand.

MARIE: If you want a gallant escort
　　find a soldier, find a soldier
　　If you want to thrill and gamble
　　take a soldier, take a soldier
　　If you want your flesh to tremble
　　tremble, tremble, tremble, tremble
　　...k a soldier, ...k a soldier.

CROWD: Vive Marie, Vive l'Amour, Vive l'Armée!

ESTERHAZY enters, a popular figure. He is cheered by the crowd. HENRY is present.

CROWD: Long live Esterhazy. Three cheers Hip-Hip-Hurrah. Long live Esterhazy. Three cheers Hip-Hip-Hurrah. Welcome. We honour you. We rejoice at your presence.

HENRY goes to ESTERHAZY and greets him. MATHIEU and PICQUART enter. ESTERHAZY looks around.

ESTERHAZY: *(To HENRY.)* You see, those bastards are following me!

MATHIEU observes ESTERHAZY. PICQUART instructs two of his secret servicemen to watch him.

MARIE: Welcome to our hero! *(Goes to ESTERHAZY and whispers in his ear.)* I want to celebrate tonight in our special way.

ESTERHAZY: *(Smacking her on the bottom.)* You irresistible wench! First I will gamble and try my luck. I need money. I am not as rich as they are. *(Looking in the direction of MATHIEU.)* Send him two old troopers. Perhaps they'll give him something he'll remember!

Two of the girls make their way to MATHIEU and begin to flirt. ESTERHAZY goes into the private gaming room. More and more noise as his losses grow and his temper gets worse. MARIE stays outside. She flirts and moves amongst the crowd to centre stage.

MARIE: Beloved guests, glorious soldiers, I present you with a new number which will be the rage of Paris. The Yids Polka.

A group of dancers perform caricatures of Jews, DREYFUS with a long nose and a matching partner (a dancer or MARIE).

MARIE: *(Refer to English translation on page 75.)*
   V'là qu'dans les rues d'Paris
   on n'trouve plus qu'des youdis
   A chaque pas sur votre chemin
   Vous n'voyez qu'des youpins.
   C'est une race de vermine
   Ils ont de tristes mines

On d'vrait les expulser
Ou bien les assomer.

ZOLA: France, how have your people succumbed to such
depths of prejudice?

MARIE: Trala la la la
La la la la la
Chassez ces coquins
Oh! les sales youpins.

CROWD: Trala la la la
Trala la la la
La la la la la
Chassez ces coquins
Oh! les sales youpins.

ESTERHAZY: *(From the gaming room.)* I need money to pay.
Give me time to pay.

MARIE: D'après leurs renseignements
Dreyfus est innocent
Mais ils sont incapables
D'découvrir le coupable.
On peut l'dire sans vergogne
Ils ont triste besogne
Quand leur race périra
Alors chacun chantera.

ZOLA: You have... you... you have allowed the rage of hatred ...

MARIE: Trala la la la
La la la la la
Chassez les coquins
Oh! les sales youpins.

CROWD: Trala la la la
La la la la la
Chassez les coquins
Oh! les sales youpins.

The CROWD becomes hysterical and begins to dance. People make antisemitic signs. ESTERHAZY comes out of the gaming room. MARIE goes up to him, but he pushes her aside. She caresses him. She leads ESTERHAZY into the Chambre Privee. She manoeuvres him to the divan and leans over him coquettishly.

MARIE: You are always running off to work, you never have time for me *(Sexily.)* Tell me my dear Count what can I do for you tonight? *(They begin to embrace. She sits up.)* Ah! There was a letter for you at home.

ESTERHAZY: Who is it from?

MARIE: *(Taking the envelope from her decollete and looking at it.)* There is no sender.

ESTERHAZY: Come here and read it to me. *(ESTERHAZY fondles her.)*

MARIE: *(Reading.)* Personal to Major Esterhazy. Your name will be the object of a great scandal. The Dreyfus family are planning to trap you. Major Picquart has bought samples of your handwriting and is passing documents to the family. They will ask you for a retrial. They will ruin you.

ESTERHAZY: *(Jumping up in panic.)* I must flee. Where is the train timetable? No, I must see Schwartzkoppen. He must save me. *(He paces up and down, then jumps into a chair. He takes a phial from his pocket.)* I will kill myself.

MARIE: *(Taking the phial from him.)* You miserable coward. If you run and desert me, I'll tell everything.

ESTERHAZY: *(Falling on his knees.)* No, no! Swear, that you will not tell, nothing, please nothing.

MARIE: A man in dark glasses called today. He said it was important. You are to meet him at five tomorrow in secret in the urinals at Parc Montsouris. *(She gives him a slip of paper).*

In Parc Montsouris. The disguised DU PATY reaches out from the urinals und beckons ESTERHAZY to follow him.

DU PATY: Do you know why we are here?

ESTERHAZY: I think so. But I do not know who you are. I am the victim of a frightful plot.

DU PATY: *(Theatrically.)* We know of the plots against you. But do not worry, you have powerful protectors.

ESTERHAZY: *(With a superior air.)* I will not allow my name to be dragged through the mud. An Esterhazy fears nothing and no one. My honour is beyond reproach. I have always acted on orders.

DU PATY: You must obey our instructions. Exercise caution! *(He leaves.)*

ESTERHAZY leaves and begins to walk home. HENRY arrives.

ESTERHAZY: I tell you we are swimming in shit, but it is not my arse that did it. I only acted on orders.

HENRY: We must clear your name.

ESTERHAZY: How?

HENRY: You must ask for a Court Martial.

ESTERHAZY: But...

HENRY: You will be acquitted. *(Cheerfully.)* Sabre in hand, we are going to charge.

HENRY/ESTERHAZY: Sabre in hand, we are going to charge, we are going to charge. Sabre in hand, we are going to charge.

They become euphoric and sing as they leave.

The street outside the Courtroom where the Court Martial of ESTERHAZY is being held. Street musicians are playing. A great crowd is gathering to hear the verdict. DRUMONT and his anti-Dreyfusard followers are present as well as a Monk and MARIE.

ZOLA is there with his Dreyfusard friends. A Rabbi and his family look on. The 'Ligue Antisemitique' and the newspaper 'La Croix' have erected stands for speakers. Violence is in the air.

STREET VENDOR: *(Vendor I)* List of Jews for sale, of Jews in French cities. List of Jews, lists...

DRUMONT mounts the stand.

STREET VENDOR: *(Vendor II)* Anti-Jewish songs, Anti-Dreyfus songs, the latest hits.

SPECTATOR: Silence! Silence for the Pope of Antisemitism!

DRUMONT: Poor Esterhazy!

CROWD: Vive Esterhazy! Down with Picquart! Down with Picquart! Vive Esterhazy!

DRUMONT: Judas sold the compassion of Christ. Dreyfus sold our nation.

CROWD: Between the Jews and us, there stands the Patrie.

The MONK approaches and stands next to DRUMONT. They compete with each other in the following tirade.

DRUMONT: The Semite is money grabbing, greedy and sly.

MONK: The Aryan is heroic, honest and naive.

DRUMONT: The Semite cannot see beyond his life on earth.

MONK: The Aryan lives with lofty thoughts of the ideal.

DRUMONT: The Semite is a trader and deceives his fellow man.

MONK: The Aryan is a poet, a monk and a soldier.

DRUMONT: The Semite exploits the Aryan, he lives like a parasite in a civilisation which he did not create.

MONK: ... which he did not create.

ZOLA: *(Unable to control himself.)* And they are your creation! Persecuted without a homeland, thrown into Ghettos like lepers.

CROWD: Down with Zola! Down with his Syndicate. Let us smash Jewish power and boot them out of France.

The crowd becomes violent and begins to stone the RABBI and his family. The anger of the Dreyfusards has been ignited. ZOLA stands up.

ZOLA: France, oh France, your people are poisoned and fanatic. Your people scream in the streets: 'Down with the Jews. Death to the Jews.' What anguish, what sadness in the souls of those who love you. Dear France, examine your conscience. Return to yourself, to the great power you are. Awake in the glory of truth and justice.

MARIE winds her way charmingly towards ZOLA. She begins almost teasingly to sing her Anti-Zola song.

MARIE: Quand donc finiras-tu, dis?
Zola d'défendr'les Youdis
Si tu n'veux plus qu'on t'emboîte
Ferm'ta boîte!
Tu n's'ras pas d'l'Académie,
Maint'nant, c'est bien entendu,
Finis donc ta comédie
T'as assez vendu!
T'as assez vendu!

Translation
When, when, shall we see the end?
of Zola defending his Yid friends?
If you don't want a kick up the arse
Shut your trap!
You'll be out of the Academy
It is now very clear,
Finish your comedy
You've betrayed us quite enough!
You've betrayed us quite enough!

CROWD: Ferm'ta boîte!
Ferm'ta boîte!
T'as assez vendu!

Translation
Shut your trap!
Shut your trap!
You've betrayed us quite enough!

MARIE: Maint'nant qu't'es rich' comm' Crésus
N'viens pas la faire aux Jésus
Ne préch'pas d'ta voix benoîte
Ferm'ta boîte!
De l'innocence de ton traître
Tu restes le seul convaincu
Au fond t'en rigol's peut-être
T'as assez vendu!
Ferm'ta boîte!
Ferm'ta boîte!
T'as assez vendu! Assez vendu!

She sticks her bottom out at ZOLA.

Translation
Now that you are rich as Croesus
Do not put blame on Jesus
Don't preach in Holy tones
Shut your trap!
Of the innocence of your traitor
You're the only one convinced
They're probably laughing at you
You've betrayed us quite enough!
Shut your trap!
Shut your trap!
You've betrayed us quite enough!

SPECTATOR: *(Exiting from the Courtroom.)* Quiet! Silence, The
Verdict! *(Heard from the Courtroom.)* In the name of the
French people! The Supreme Court Martial of the Military

Government of Paris declares unanimously, that Major Walsin Esterhazy is Not Guilty.

CROWD: Vive Esterhazy. Vive l'Armée.

People begin to exit from the Courtroom. ESTERHAZY appears.

CROWD: Vive Esterhazy, the Martyr of the Jews! Long live Esterhazy.

ESTERHAZY is congratulated. MARIE kisses him. MATHIEU and PICQUART come out of the Courtroom.

CROWD: Down with Zola! Down with Picquart! Down, down, down with them both, down with Zola and Picquart!

The crowd begins to stone MATHIEU, PICQUART and ZOLA. PICQUART is arrested. ZOLA begins to assert his authority.

ZOLA: J'Accuse, J'Accuse, J'Accuse.

As ZOLA dominates the stage, the crowd fades away dispersing into the darkness.

ZOLA: I accuse the Ministers of War, the Courts, the Generals and all who collaborated with them. I accuse them, I accuse them of being the diabolical agents of a judicial error and defending their deadly work with revolting cunning. I accuse them, I accuse them, I accuse them of being scoundrels and holding an enquiry of monstrous partiality. I have but one passion, a passion for life, in the name of humanity that has suffered and has a right to happiness. My burning protest is the cry of my soul.

The Boulevards. Street musicians. More and more people come on stage. Open conflicts, shouting of antisemitic slogans, stoning and breaking of shops. An antisemitic army assembles carrying clubs, iron bars, etc. They burn an effigy of DREYFUS and sing the anti-Jewish Marseillaise.

CROWD: *(Refer to English translation on page 70.)*
Tremblez, youpins, et vous, perfides,
L'opprobre de tous les partis,

Contre nous de la juiverie
Le troupeau hurlant s'est levé *(bis)*.

Français, pour nous, ah! quel outrage
D'être insultés par ces bandits,
Balayons donc tous ces youdis
Que notre faiblesse encourage.

Aux armes, antijuifs, formez vos bataillons.
Marchons, marchons,
Qu'un sang impur abreuve nos sillons.

The crowd follows the antisemitic marchers.

The office of the new Minister of War CAVAIGNAC slowly becomes visible. Present are BOISDEFFRE, GONSE and others. The Minister sits at his desk. They are examining HENRY's forgery. ZOLA's voice is heard from afar.

ZOLA: J'Accuse! J'Accuse!

HENRY enters. The MINISTER beckons him to come and give evidence.

MINISTER: Did you forge a letter?

HENRY: No, I did not.

MINISTER: Then what did you do?

HENRY: I just arranged some sentences.

MINISTER: No, you forged a whole letter. Confess it.

HENRY: I swear I did not.

MINISTER: Tell us the whole truth. Confess it!

HENRY: I just added some words.

MINISTER: Which words? Tell me.

HENRY: Words, which had nothing to do with this matter.

MINISTER: You received a letter. You discarded its text and added another.

HENRY: *(Demolished.)* Yes. *(As he is led out.)* I have always done my duty. I would do it again. It was for the good of the army. I am doomed. They are abandoning me.

BOISDEFFRE: Monsieur le Ministre, I do not feel well.

GONSE: Monsieur le Ministre, I do not feel well.

BOISDEFFRE/GONSE: We have the honour of asking you to accept our resignation. Vive la France, Vive l'Armée, Glory to France.

SOLDIER: *(Rushing into the room.)* Henry is dead! He has committed suicide.

The office of CAVAIGNAC fades away. LUCIE dominates the stage and petitions the Supreme Court of Appeal.

LUCIE: Slowly and painfully light has been shed on a denial of justice. The truth has emerged. It only remains to proclaim it. From the depth of human pain and with eyes that have no more tears to shed, I turn to you, for this act of final justice. I await it, as a glittering testimony to your high and impartial justice. I await it, as a word of deliverance for this loyal person who, hounded to his prison cell by implacable hatred, has submitted to his torture without weakness. I await it, as a breath of life for my failing heart so crushed by the savage anger which surrounds it.

MATHIEU: *(Arriving.)* The verdict has been annulled. There will be fresh proceedings against Alfred. The trial will be held in Rennes. *(He leaves.)*

LUCLE: *(Ecstatically.)* Alfred, you are coming home!

The Courtroom in Rennes. The Guard of 'Dishonour' arrive. They turn their backs to DREYFUS as he is marched into Court. As he enters, the spectators break into a gasp. He has become an old, old man of 39. He is pale and strained. He wears the uniform of the artillery. He has difficulty in walking. He stumbles. His uniform flaps around him.

Seven Judges are present. Large figure of Christ on the wall. DREYFUS salutes the president with his white-gloved hand, takes off his kepi and sits. MERCIER watches everything. He controls the military. He mounts the witness stand.

MERCIER: I swear to speak the truth, nothing but the truth. I hold that the motive for Dreyfus's treason was that he has no feelings of patriotism.

DREYFUS watches MERCIER with intensity.

MERCIER: He was once heard to say when a patriot was lamenting the Alsace Lorraine: 'For us Jews it is not the same, in whatever country we are our G-d is with us.' The treason is clearly evidenced by the prisoner's contradictions and lies and from the technical examination of the Bordereau. I have not reached my age without learning that all that is human is fallible. I am an honest man and the son of an honest man. Since the campaign for a re-trial began I have followed closely all the discussion. If the slightest doubt had crossed my mind, I should be the first to declare and to say before Captain Dreyfus: 'I have been honestly mistaken' ...

DREYFUS here electrifies the Court. Losing all self-control he virtually hurls himself at MERCIER and cries out in a voice like a wounded animal

DREYFUS: That is what you ought to say!

MERCIER is taken aback and blanches - DREYFUS is forced back into his seat by the guards.

MERCIER: I would say, I have been honestly mistaken. I would acknowledge it and do all that is possible to right a terrible mistake.

DREYFUS again in that same unforgettable voice.

DREYFUS: It is your duty to do so!

MERCIER: Well, it is not so. My conviction has not changed since 1894. It has been strengthened by the most thorough study of the Dossier and the utter uselessness of all the efforts to prove the prisoner's innocence.

JUDGE: *(Presiding.)* The Court will now consider its verdict.

The Judges leave to consider their verdict. There is commotion in Court. Shortly, the Judges return. They raise their hands to their caps in Military salute.

JUDGE: *(Presiding.)* In the name of the French people. Is Alfred Dreyfus, Captain in the Artillery, guilty of having dealings with a foreign power and delivering the documents listed in the 'Bordereau'?

JUDGE: Guilty.

JUDGE: Not guilty.

JUDGE: Guilty.

JUDGE: *(Presiding.)* Not guilty.

JUDGE: Guilty.

JUDGE: Guilty.

JUDGE: Guilty.

JUDGE: *(Presiding.)* The Court declares by a majority of five votes to two that the accused is Guilty. Alfred Dreyfus you have been found Guilty... *(His voice is drowned by the crowd.)*

The Courtroom begins to empty. ZOLA, LUCIE and PICQUART are stunned.

LUCIE: I feel terror, sacred terror.

PICQUART: I feel terror.

ZOLA: I feel the sacred terror of rivers flowing back to their source,

LUCIE: Of the earth turning without a sun.

PICQUART: Never has there been a more detestable monument of human infamy.

LUCIE: Human infamy.

ZOLA: Even Jesus was condemned but once

PICQUART: Even Jesus

LUCIE: Jesus even.

The Dreyfusards have gathered near the cell of DREYFUS. LUCIE and MATHIEU enter the prison cell area. MATHIEU looks at his brother whose pretended calm hides an inner suffering so atrocious that MATHIEU finds it difficult to control his emotions. LUCIE stifles her tears.

LUCIE: *(To MATHIEU.)* I am frightened. He wants to see his children. Just once more.

MATHIEU: *(To LUCIE.)* We must accept a pardon to save his life.

DREYFUS: *(Overhearing, disturbed.)* A Pardon? That would be my final degradation.

LUCIE: Your children will grow up fatherless, oppressed by the questions they cannot answer. My years alone have drained me of life.

DREYFUS: My innocence has been my nourishment. The innocence was my nourishment. My liberty is nothing for me without honour. I declare that my innocence is absolute.

LUCIE: His innocence is absolute.

DREYFUS: Until my dying breath I will fight, fight for its recognition.

LUCIE: I will fight for its recognition. His innocence is absolute.

DREYFUS: My innocence is absolute.

DEMANGUE returns with an authority for the release of DREYFUS. It is handed to the PRISON DIRECTOR. The gates of the cell are opened. LUCIE and DREYFUS approach each other and collapse into each others arms.

ZOLA: *(From backstage.)* The day will come when the truth will be understood by all.

DREYFUS is now quite alone at the back of the stage. He begins to walk slowly to the front. His walk is interrupted by memories and associations. Figures, musical themes and sounds from his past life are seen and heard – the Degradation, the Rennes verdict, the declaration of his innocence, his re-integration into the army. Finally, the ceremony of the Legion of Honour – the General touches DREYFUS on his shoulder three times with his sword and pins the cross on his black dolman. DREYFUS arrives at the front of the stage. He is old and frail. He salutes the Tricolore. The voice of DREYFUS as a boy (tape) is heard.

THE BOY DREYFUS: Papa. When I grow up I want to be a soldier.

END

Dreyfus after his return from Devil's Island